THE OSCAR DIRECTORS

Moviemaking is justly considered "a director's medium." It is an art form largely controlled by the vision, taste, skill, and inspiration of each film's director. Directors influence the final form the script will take; approve all locations, sets, costumes; guide each actor through every scene; and oversee the editing to the very last frame. If a motion picture "belongs" to any one person it is the director, who is responsible for virtually every aspect of its creation.

It is therefore surprising that although many books have been written about various actors and films that have won Oscars, no book has ever been devoted to Oscar-winning directors. I. G. Edmonds and Reiko Mimura—experts who have published other works on cinema—have impressively rectified this omission with *The Oscar Directors*.

Every director honored with an Academy Award is described in a concise biography and his style is cogently evaluated. A list of other notable films each winner directed provides additional insight into the development of cinematic techniques that have distinguished the work of the great moviemakers.

All fifty-three winners of the Oscar for directing are presented, in chronological order from Frank Borzage and Louis Milestone in 1927-28 to Robert Benton in 1979. More than 200 illustrations, including pictures of each director and stills from their renowned movies, help make this book both a comprehensive reference work and a volume sure to evoke nostalgic contemplation in every true film fan.

The Oscar Directors offers entertaining and enlightening reading to anyone interested in the special role directors' creative genius has played in motion picture history.

ALSO BY I.G. EDMONDS

Big U Universal in the Silent Days
Second Sight
Buddhism
Motorcycle Racing for Beginners

ALSO WITH REIKO MIMURA

Paramount Pictures and the People Who Made Them

THE OSCAR DIRECTORS

I.G. Edmonds
Reiko Mimura

The Tantivy Press
Magdalen House
136-148 Tooley Street
London, SE1 2TT, England

First Edition
Manufactured in the United States of America
For information write to A. S. Barnes and Company, Inc.,
P.O. Box 3051, San Diego, CA 92038

Library of Congress Cataloging In Publication Data

Edmonds, I G
The Oscar Directors.

Includes index.
1. Moving-picture producers and directors — United States. 2. Academy awards (moving pictures) 3. Moving-pictures — United States. I. Mimura, Reiko, joint author. II. Title.
PM1998.A2E33 791.43′0233′0922 79-21294
ISBN 0-498-02444-X

1 2 3 4 5 6 7 8 9 84 83 82 81 80

To Oliver Dernberger

Once again, Oliver, prince of movie historians, was an indispensable aid to us in probing obscure points in film history.

Contents

Acknowledgments

The majority of illustrations are from the authors' own collections. Grateful acknowledgment for assistance in finding others is made to Oliver Dernberger, Leonard Brown, Malcolm Willetts, Kenneth G. Lawrence, *Movie Star News*, and Larry Edmunds Book Shop. Special mention should also be made of the courteous assistance in the basic research given by the staff of the Margaret Herrick Library of the Academy of Motion Picture Arts and Science.

Introduction

DIRECTORS AND OSCARS

It would seem logical that the best motion picture of the year would naturally have the best director, stars, writers and technicians. However, the membership of the Academy of Motion Picture Arts and Sciences, bestowers of the coveted statuette known as the Oscar, have never seen it that way.

As members of the profession, they presumably judge pictures, performances and technical achievements from a viewpoint different from those who participate in movies from the other side of the screen. Of course, it is only fair to admit that there have been disgruntled people who claim the choices are made the same way some pick their racehorses: the voters close their eyes and stick a pin in the list.

In fifty-two years of academy presentations, only twice has any picture made a complete sweep of the top four award categories: best picture, best director, best actor, and best actress. The first to achieve this was *It Happened One Night* (1934). In addition to best picture, it brought honors to director Frank Capra and stars Clark Gable and Claudette Colbert. The second top sweep was made by *One Flew Over the Cuckoo's Nest* (1975), forty-one years later. The director was Milos Forman, with Jack Nicholson and Louise Fletcher winning Oscars for best actor and actress.

Directors and best pictures have paired together better. In fifty-three times at the post, best picture and best director have teamed thirty-seven times. They are:

Lewis Milestone and *All Quiet on the Western Front*, 1929–1930.
Frank Lloyd and *Cavalcade*, 1932–1933.
Frank Capra and *It Happened One Night*, 1934.
Frank Capra and *You Can't Take It with You*, 1938.
Victor Fleming and *Gone with the Wind*, 1939.
John Ford and *How Green Was My Valley*, 1941.
William Wyler and *Mrs. Miniver*, 1942.
Michael Curtiz and *Casablanca*, 1943.

Leo McCarey and *Going My Way*, 1944.
Billy Wilder and *The Lost Weekend*, 1945.
William Wyler and *The Best Years of Our Lives*, 1946.
Elia Kazan and *Gentleman's Agreement*, 1947.
Joseph L. Mankiewicz for *All about Eve*, 1950.
Fred Zinnemann for *From Here to Eternity*, 1953.
Elia Kazan for *On the Waterfront*, 1954.
Delbert Mann for *Marty*, 1955.
David Lean for *The Bridge on the River Kwai*, 1957.
Vincente Minnelli for *Gigi*, 1958.
William Wyler for *Ben Hur*, 1959.
Billy Wilder for *The Apartment*, 1960.
Robert Wise for *West Side Story*, 1961.
David Lean for *Lawrence of Arabia*, 1962.
Tony Richardson for *Tom Jones*, 1963.
George Cukor for *My Fair Lady*, 1964.
Robert Wise for *The Sound of Music*, 1965.
Fred Zinnemann for *A Man for All Seasons*, 1966.
Carol Reed for *Oliver!*, 1968.
John Schlesinger for *Midnight Cowboy*, 1969.
Franklin J. Schaffner for *Patton*, 1970.
William Friedkin for *The French Connection*, 1971.
George Roy Hill for *The Sting*, 1973.
Francis Ford Coppola for *The Godfather II*, 1974.
Milos Forman for *One Flew Over the Cuckoo's Nest*, 1975.
John Avildsen for *Rocky*, 1976.
Woody Allen for *Annie Hall*, 1977.
Michael Cimino for *The Deer Hunter*, 1978.
Robert Benton for *Kramer vs Kramer*, 1979.

In the past twenty years, only twice have the best picture awards failed to pull their directors along with them for an additional Oscar. In 1967, the director's award went to Mike Nichols for *The Graduate*, but *In the Heat of the Night* took best picture honors. *The Godfather* was deservedly the best picture of 1972, but Bob Fosse took the director's honors for *Cabaret*.

As we look over the pictures for which directors won Oscars, we do not see a really bad picture in the list. Only two of them did not do well at the box office, *Cavalcade* and *The Informer*, although both were critical successes. Commenting on *Cavalcade*'s poor audience response, William C. deMille commented, "The public does not want literate pictures."

While the academy voters never picked a poor picture, can we say that they always picked the best picture? Here we can get into a lot of controversy.

The very first director's award went to Frank Borzage for *Seventh Heaven*, a classic picture. But was it better than *Wings*, *The Last Command* or *Underworld*? They were released in the same voting period. Until 1934, the judging was done by seasons, which began in August of each year and ran through the next July.

Seventh Heaven was a great popular success, but *Wings*, the first of the aviation epics, was better liked by the public and also got the first Oscar for best picture. On the other hand, *The Last Command*, with Emil Jannings as the Russian general who ended as a Hollywood extra, has enjoyed the greater critical success through the years.

Looking back over the fifty-three-year history of the Oscar, quite a lot of us will, no doubt, question some of the voters' choices. Take 1937 for example: Leo McCarey took the director's Oscar for *The Awful Truth*. This was a very fine comedy, but 1937 was also the year of *Captains Courageous, Dead End, The Good Earth, Lost Horizon*, and the first version of *A Star Is Born*. Was *The Awful Truth* a better-directed picture than these? It seems very likely that today's voters would probably pick *A Star Is Born* and director William Wellman for the honor.

It is hard to find a pattern in the academy's vote for best director. The pictures varied widely in technique and subject. Few had a message. Few had any cinematic innovations. However, all told good stories. So it would appear that the academy voters made their choices the same way audiences do: they picked what they liked. And their choices often reflected the trends of the times.

Gentleman's Agreement (1947) is a case in point. It was not the best picture of the year and not the best directed either, although it took Oscars for both. Competing pictures and directors were George Cukor and *A Double Life*; Edward Dmytryk for *Crossfire*, Henry Coster for *The Bishop's Wife*, and David Lean for *Great Expectations*. One would favor Cukor or Lean in this case. However, *Gentleman's Agreement* was the first major picture to tackle the problem of anti-Semitism, and this novelty worked in the picture's favor. It was a picture with a message—an important message basically, but so weakly presented as to be almost no message at all. Of course, we have to consider that even to venture into the fray, no matter how timidly, was a genuine act of courage in those days. And this is what brought in the votes.

Another question is, how much credit do the directors deserve? In some cases, all credit is earned by the director-producer who has the strength and box-office record to enforce his demands upon cast and studio, such as Wyler or Wilder. Then there is the question of films like *Gone with the Wind*, in which the producer interfered inordinately and then claimed the credit. In this case, we can only point out that if *Gone with the Wind* had not been released in 1939, Victor Fleming may well have won the director's Oscar anyway for the splendid *The Wizard of Oz*.

So let us argue no more about the merits of the decisions. The winners were all good pictures and good entertainment.

Most books on the Academy Awards have concentrated primarily upon the best pictures and the best actors and actresses. Although the claim is often made that the director is the real magnetic force that draws together the scattered parts to make a picture, he has been given scant notice in such books. The pictures and the stars are the important things because these are what interest the general public. Therefore, this book was written to acknowledge the directors who have won Oscars for their work.

Unfortunately, when one deals with fifty-three different director awards and an equal number of films, there is not sufficient room to say much about each.

This has caused the authors to be briefer than they would have liked. With but a few exceptions, all of these directors deserve a full book of their own, if one has not yet been written.

The original intention was to include a picture of the director and three stills from his winning picture. However, the final decision was to use one still from the picture that won the director's award and supplementary pictures to show other and contrasting examples of his work. In this way, we hoped to show the director's versatility.

THE OSCAR DIRECTORS

Frank Borzage was the first director to win an Oscar from the newly created Academy of Motion Picture Arts and Sciences.

1927-1928:

Frank Borzage for Seventh Heaven

Frank Borzage (1893–1962), a veteran who had been around the Hollywood scene since 1915, was the first director honored by the newly formed Academy of Motion Picture Arts and Sciences.

There is some confusion about his ancestry. He has been reported as both Swedish and Italian-Swiss. In any event, Borzage was born in Salt Lake City, Utah, one of fourteen children of a stonecutter. He left school at thirteen to work in the Park City mines, but quit at sixteen when a traveling show offered him a place at a dollar a day. His father, after threatening to disown him if he left, gave Borzage fifty dollars and told him to write home if he got stranded.

Within a short time, the troupe manager had borrowed Borzage's fifty dollars; and, in an even shorter time after that, the troupe was stranded. Too proud to write home so soon, he lived as best he could until another company took him on as a "utility man." He thought that meant doing whatever acting job came up. What it really meant was speaking ten lines of dialogue on stage, with the rest of his time spent getting props, moving sets, and arranging transportation for the rest of the troupe.

As time went by, Borzage began specializing in character roles. Then Thomas H. Ince hired him for the Kay Bee Company and thought Frank's curly hair and dimpled chin were better suited to a leading man. He worked for Ince, Universal, and Famous Players. At Famous, one of his films was the lead opposite Mae Murray in *A Mormon Maid* (1916) with Hobart Bosworth and Edythe Chapman. Soon after this, he began directing. He did well enough to get by, but made no real impression until he filmed *Toton* (1919) with Olive Thomas, an ex-Follies girl with the little-girl charm that Janet Gaynor later displayed.

The following year, he made *Humoresque*, with Gaston Glass, Alma Rubens, and Vera Gordon, which solidified his reputation as a master of sentimental drama. In the next few years, he directed some of the screen's top stars: Alma Rubens and Lew Cody in *The Valley of Silent Men* (1922), Colleen Moore in *The Nth Commandment* (1923), Norma Talmadge in *Secrets* (1924), and then, in 1927, he made *Seventh Heaven*.

The story of *Seventh Heaven* is not much. It was based upon the stage success by Austin Strong, who wrote *Three Wise Fools*. The stage production starred Helen Mencken as Diane. Borzage wanted her for the movie role, but Winfield Sheehan, Fox's studio manager, insisted on Janet Gaynor. Janet had made five pictures, none of which was very good, but Sheehan liked her; also, her salary was less than Mencken's.

Charles Farrell had the role of Chico, a Parisian sewer cleaner whose ambition was to advance to street cleaner. He does not doubt that he will succeed, for, as he says, "I am a very remarkable fellow!" However, he is disillusioned by religion. At one time, he burned candles and prayed for a blond girl—but got nothing for his trouble. Then he happens upon Diane being beaten by her vengeful sister (Gladys Brockwell) because Diane resists being drawn into a life then described as a fate worse than death.

Chico takes her to his garret room. The police come for her, on a runaway complaint from her sister, but Chico puts them off by claiming that Diane is now his wife. The two come to love each other in the idealistic and sentimental manner for which Borzage had become famous. Chico's attic room becomes a seventh heaven to these two childlike people.

In his acting days, Borzage played opposite Mae Murray in *A Mormon Maid* (1916). Copyright 1916 by Famous Players Film Company.

Eugene O'Brien and Norma Talmadge were in Borzage's 1924 success, *Secrets*. Copyright 1924 by First National Pictures.

Janet Gaynor and Charles Farrell, as Diane and Chico, find *Seventh Heaven* in their childlike love for each other. Copyright 1927 by Fox Film Corporation.

Then the drums of war begin beating and Chico goes off to fight the Germans in World War I. The two lovers lose touch with each other. Chico is blinded in battle and comes back to Paris believing that the world has ended for him. But Diane has been waiting. She finds him, and the lovers are reunited.

Henry King remade the film in 1937 with Simone Simon and James Stewart. It lacked the punch of the original, perhaps because King lacked Borzage's ability to make a fairy tale seem real.

Seventh Heaven (1927), released by Fox Film Corporation. Directed by Frank Borzage. Screenplay by Benjamin Glazer, from the play by Austin Strong. Photographed by Ernest Palmer. Principal cast members: Janet Gaynor, Charles Farrell, Ben Bard, Gladys Brockwell, Marie Mosquini, David Butler, Albert Gran, George Stone.

Lewis Milestone was twice awarded the Academy Award for best director. Copyright 1930 by Universal Pictures Corporation.

1927-1928

Lewis Milestone for Two Arabian Knights

In its first year of awards, the Academy of Motion Picture Arts and Sciences was still feeling its way. Somehow, the idea got around that directing a comedy was different from directing drama. So the first awards split the direction award into a regular and a comedy category. The idea that the two are poles apart may have come from observing the diverging styles of men like Mack Sennett and Cecil B. DeMille.

The comedy award for best direction went to Lewis Milestone (b. 1895), who had been knocking around Hollywood since the end of World War I. It was the Russian Revolution that sent twenty-two-year-old Milestone fleeing to the United States. He immediately joined the United States Army, having heard that this was a shortcut to citizenship. Mustered out of the service in 1919, he headed for Hollywood with a vague idea of becoming a writer.

Movies had now become big time and thousands of others had the similar idea of gaining a foothold in the glamorous industry. Milestone found himself one of a mob of hopefuls. He made a few friends among them. One was an ex-aviator named William Wellman, who got in through a wartime acquaintance with Douglas Fairbanks, but who was not doing so well right then. Another as poorly situated as Milestone was William K. Howard, later to become a prominent director himself.

By 1920, Milestone had opened the gate. There are several stories as to how he did it. One says flatly that Hollywood finally recognized his genius. This version was attributed in 1930 to Milestone (who was then making *All Quiet on the Western Front*). Another account says it was William Wellman who got Milestone in. Still another story said that Milestone convinced Carl Laemmle that he was Uncle Carl's long-lost nephew from Germany. Laemmle had a reputation for taking care of European relatives. Two of these stories might be partially true, but William Wellman was in no position to help anyone right then.

In any event, Milestone became an assistant cutter and then a writer. He graduated to directing in 1925 with *Seven Sinners* and went on to make several pictures for Paramount. Then he met one of the oddest characters in Hollywood history, Howard Hughes. Hughes had just brought his Texas millions to Hollywood with the idea of making pictures.

Milestone became Hughes's director, handling Thomas Meighan in *The New Klondike* (1926). This impressed Hughes enough to keep Milestone for *Two Arabian Knights*, which would be released by United Artists. This picture brought Milestone the 1927–1928 Academy Award for best achievement in comedy direction—an award that was given only this one time.

The story was about Private Phelps (William Boyd) and Sergeant McGaffney (Louis Wolheim) in a plot that was somewhat like what would pop up years later in the Crosby-Hope Road pictures. In this one, the boys are captured by the Germans. They manage to escape by disguising themselves as Arabs, and stow away on a ship bound for Jaffa.

The plot pot begins to boil when they discover an Arabian princess aboard. Phelps makes quite a hit with the princess (Mary Astor), but a spy tells Prince Shevket (Ian Keith), the princess's boy friend. He has the boys jailed, but the American consul in Jaffa gets them out. Shevket wants to fight a duel with Phelps but cannot because of the soldier's "low" station. So the emir conveniently makes the boys knights so Shevket can slice Phelps up in a legal duel. In Arabian Nights fashion, Phelps and McGaffney heroically baffle the plotters, foil their would-be murderer, and escape with the lovely princess.

William Boyd and Louis Wolheim had roles a lot like those of Crosby and Hope in their "road" pictures when they made *Two Arabian Knights*, which Lewis Milestone directed for Howard Hughes's Caddo Productions. Copyright 1927 by Caddo Productions.

An excellent in-depth set for *The Racket* provided production value for another film Lewis Milestone made for Howard Hughes. The film starred Thomas Meighan. Copyright 1928 by Caddo Productions and Paramount Pictures, Incorporated.

Lewis Milestone did the best he could with the 1932 remake of *Rain*, but Joan Crawford was neither a Gloria Swanson nor a Jeanne Eagles. Copyright 1932 by United Artists Corporation.

When the first Academy Awards were handed out, Milestone was in competition for the comedy director's award with Charles Chaplin for *The Circus*, and Ted Wilde for Harold Lloyd's *Speedy*. Now this was about as formidable competition as one could ask for, and it is a tribute to Milestone's ability that he won.

Two Arabian Knights (1927), produced by Caddo Productions for United Artists Corporation release. Directed by Lewis Milestone, with supervision by Howard Hughes and John W. Considine, Jr. Screenplay by James T. O'Donohue and Wallace Smith. Photography by Tony Gaudio. Cast included, Mary Astor, William (Bill) Boyd, Louis Wolheim, Ian Keith.

Frank Lloyd won the director's Oscar twice. His career began as an actor for Universal in 1913. Copyright 1933 by Fox Film Corporation.

1928-1929

Frank Lloyd
for The Divine Lady

Geraldine Farrar is quoted as saying that Frank Lloyd (1889–1960) was better with ships than people. Opera singer Farrar starred in Lloyd's 1921 film *The World and Its Women*. It is hard to argue with someone who was there. But, in this case, we fear that "Gerry" libeled a fine director.

It is true that Lloyd was noted for his sea pictures; he made the 1924 version of Sabatini's *The Sea Hawk* with Milton Sills. Then he took the second Academy Award for directing with *The Divine Lady*, the story of Lord Nelson's sea battles, and the famous *Mutiny on the Bounty* (1935) with Charles Laughton and Clark Gable. In between, he made a number of less notable sea pictures, including *The Ruler of the Seas* (1940) with Douglas Fairbanks Jr., and *The Eagle of the Sea* (1926) with Florence Vidor and Ricardo Cortez, among others.

But, although noted for sea dramas, Lloyd made every kind of picture, directing more than seventy features and hundreds of shorts in his long career. His films always combined good action with excellent sets that displayed his cast to good advantage. It is all very well for Josef von Sternberg to dismiss Lloyd with a condescending, "He was a usually good commercial director," but Hollywood thought enough of Lloyd to give him the best director's Oscar twice. This is an honor Von Sternberg never achieved once.

Lloyd started in films in 1913, working as an actor and then as an actor-director for Carl Laemmle at Universal. He switched from shorts to features in 1916, directing such pictures as *A Tale of Two Cities* (1917), with William Farnum, and *The Rainbow Trail* (1918), with William Farnum, a Zane Grey thriller which was later a Tom Mix hit. Other notable Lloyd films were *Madame X* (1921), with Blanche Sweet, *Oliver Twist* (1922), with Jackie Coogan as Oliver and Lon Chaney, Sr., giving a superb performance as Fagin, *Ashes of Vengeance* (1923), with Norma Talmadge, and *The Sea Hawk* (1924), with Milton Sills. Also in 1924, Lloyd made *The Black Oxen*, with Corrine Griffith and Clara Bow.

Miss Griffith, "the orchid of the screen," was back with Lloyd for *The Divine Lady* (1928), with Victor Varconi as a brooding Lord Nelson. This film brought Lloyd the second Oscar awarded for dramatic direction.

The Divine Lady is the story of Emma Hamilton who started out as an artist's model, becoming wife of a British ambassador, and then mistress of Lord Nelson, the great sea captain. During the Napoleonic wars, Nelson was bitterly criticized for seeming to neglect the war for Lady Hamilton's bedchamber. There is some truth in the charge. However, Lady Hamilton had powerful political connections and was able to further Nelson's career.

Subsequently, Nelson lost an eye and an arm in battle. He turned one infirmity to his advantage. In the battle of Copenhagen, he was second in command. The commander raised signal flags ordering a withdrawal. Nelson put the telescope to his blind eye and said, "I don't see any signals!" He went on to a glorious victory, and was killed later in the Battle of Trafalgar. His last words to his lieutenant were, "Take care of poor Lady Hamilton!"

Lloyd focused more on the romance than upon the wars, but this was what audiences of the day wanted. Lloyd gave them romance and beauty (for the film was handsomely mounted), so they forgave him for killing off the hero in the last reel.

Corrine Griffith and Marie Dressler were in Lloyd's *The Divine Lady*, the film that brought the director the 1928–1929 Oscar. Copyright 1928 by First National Pictures.

Talking pictures were taking over when the Academy Awards were handed out. They almost swept the board. *The Divine Lady* and Ernest Lubitsch's *The Patriot*, with Emil Jannings, were the only silents to get major nominations. *The Broadway Melody* took top picture honors. Mary Pickford in *Coquette* and Warner Baxter in *In Old Arizona* were the best actress and actor. Frank Lloyd's Oscar for directing *The Divine Lady* and Clyde De Vinna's cinematography on *White Shadows in the South Seas* (with Monte Blue in a W.S. Van Dyke film) were the only silents to win major awards.

The talkies were taking over.

One of Frank Lloyd's early films was Zane Grey's *The Rainbow Trail* with William Farnum and Ann Forrest. Copyright 1918 by Fox Film Corporation.

Milton Sills offers the corsairs all the rest of the loot in exchange for Enid Bennett in Frank Lloyd's *The Sea Hawk*. Copyright 1924 by First National Pictures.

The Divine Lady (1929), released by First National Pictures. Produced and directed by Frank Lloyd. Screenplay based upon E. Barrington's (L. Adams Beck) novel. Photographed by John Seitz. Principal cast members: Corrine Griffith, Victor Varconi, H.B. Warner, Marie Dressler.

After winning the first Academy Award for comedy direction, Lewis Milestone proved equally adept at drama with *All Quiet on the Western Front.*

1929-1930

Lewis Milestone
for All Quiet on the Western Front

Carl Laemmle, the eccentric head of Universal Pictures, was born in Germany and never lost his love for his fatherland. At the end of World War I, he was the first to send relief money and supplies to his home town. And he constantly pushed for Americans to forget the resentments and hatreds of the war and for them to understand the German people.

So, when *All Quiet on the Western Front* by Erich Maria Remarque was published in 1929, Laemmle was the only Hollywood producer who would consider making a film that showed German soldiers sympathetically. Laemmle was told that the American Legion would picket the theaters that showed such a film, even if patriotic Americans did not burn the places down first.

However, Carl Laemmle, Jr., wanted to make it. The elder Laemmle looked upon his twenty-one-year-old son as another genius like Irving Thalberg. The pro-German slant also appealed to Laemmle. He supported Junior after a survey by Paul Gulick, of Universal's publicity staff, reported that sentiment against the book was not as strong as some were claiming.

Junior Laemmle picked Lewis Milestone to direct the film. He knew Milestone had been a soldier and felt he could understand the characters. The result was one of the classic films of the screen, and the first real antiwar film. Thomas H. Ince tried to make an antiwar film with *Civilization* in 1916 and failed. Both *The Big Parade* (1925) and *What Price Glory?* (1926) were also supposed to be antiwar, but the cheers outweighed the brief flashes of war horrors. *All Quiet on the Western Front* showed war for what it is—boredom, butchery, and bombast.

The film had no stars and needed none. The story revolves around Paul Baumer (Lew Ayres). He is inspired to join the army after a rousing patriotic speech by his schoolteacher. Disillusionment comes fast. The training camp is a prison of boredom, service is a constant humiliation and following these is the shocking horror of the battlefield.

Death and the callousness of battlefield hospitals increase Baumer's sense of desperation. The only humanity he encounters is the old sergeant, Katczinsky (Louis Wolheim). Finally, Baumer is wounded and sent home to recuperate. His mother's solicitude sickens him. He wanders back to his old school and finds the fanatically patriotic teacher extolling the virtues of war to another group of youngsters. Paul interrupts to tell the truth. He is denounced by the teacher and hooted at as a coward by the students.

Paul goes back to his company. War has taken its toll. Of those he knew, only Sergeant Katczinsky remains. New cannon fodder has replaced those who came up with Paul in the beginning. Soon the sergeant is killed, leaving Paul feeling completely alone although surrounded by an army of men. Then, one quiet day during a lull in the fighting, Paul sees a butterfly outside the trench. He rises to grab it. A French sniper sees him and he is shot. The book ends here with a quote from the day's dispatch: "All quiet on the western front." Milestone added an epilogue to be sure the audience got his point. It showed ghostly soldiers marching off into the mists of oblivion. Their faces are sad as they look back accusingly at the audience.

Everything about the film is superb. Milestone got exceptional performances from his cast, and his treatment of the battle scenes, done with a fluid camera, was hailed at the time as the best ever made. They still hold up well when viewed today.

Milestone went on to make a wide variety of pictures: *The Front Page* (1931), *The General Dies at Dawn* (1936), *Anything Goes* (1936), *Of Mice and Men* (1939), and *Pork Chop Hill* (1939), but he never again achieved the power of *All Quiet on the Western Front.*

Lew Ayres was Paul, Louis Wolheim was Katczinsky, and Ben Alexander played Kammerich in Lewis Milestone's antiwar drama *All Quiet on the Western Front.* Copyright 1930 by Universal Pictures Corporation.

Gary Cooper and Madeline Carroll were the stars of *The General Died at Dawn,* directed by Lewis Milestone in 1936. Akim Tamiroff, center, is the general of the title. Copyright 1936 by Paramount Pictures Corporation.

Why? The answer may lie in an article Milestone wrote in 1959: He blamed the decline of some famous directors upon the producer system which took away freedom of action from the director. Milestone said, "They couldn't function. They were forced to go along with the system and they went." Milestone was one of those who chose to go along with the system.

All Quiet on the Western Front (1930), produced by Carl Laemmle, Jr., for Universal Pictures Corporation release. Directed by Lewis Milestone. Screenplay by Del Andrews, Maxwell Anderson, and George Abbott, from the novel by Erich Maria Remarque. Photographed by Arthur Edeson. Dialogue directed by George Cukor. Principal cast members: Lew Ayres, Louis Wolheim, John Wray, Slim Summerville, William Bakewell.

Anything Goes **(1936), starring a young Bing Crosby, is quite a contrast in directorial style from Lewis Milestone's Oscar-winning *All Quiet on the Western Front.* Copyright 1936 by Paramount Pictures Corporation.**

Norman Taurog tries to get Judy Garland to tone down a bit during the filming of *Presenting Lily Mars*. Copyright 1942 by Metro-Goldwyn-Mayer.

1930-1931

Norman Taurog for Skippy

Norman Taurog (b. 1902) was born of actor parents in Chicago. He followed the family profession, becoming one of the children in David Belasco's *A Good Little Devil* with Ernest Truex and Mary Pickford.

Later, Taurog played for seventy-nine weeks in the Jewish comedy *Potash and Perlmutter*. Then, at sixteen, King Baggott, the director-actor, got Taurog some minor parts at Universal Pictures.

Taurog had always been fat, and there was not much demand for his type in Universal's New York studio. Baggott arranged for the boy to go to Hollywood where the bulk of Universal's films were made. Here Grace Cunard and Francis Ford, John Ford's brother, gave him some work.

There was still not much demand for a fat teenager. So Taurog became a property man, and later began directing comedies. After he was seasoned on two-reelers, he was advanced to directing features.

Taurog was never a great director, but he was jolly and a delight to work with. Everyone liked him and his sets were one big fun house. He believed in giving the public entertainment. Symbolism, allegory, cinematic tricks, and social content were left to others.

In an interview late in his career, Taurog said, "Give the public comedy and musicals and you are pretty sure of giving them what they want."

That is exactly what Taurog gave them. As a result, he is ignored by critics and those who write about the films of the 30s to the 60s (Taurog was active until 1967). This despite his leading Spencer Tracy to an Academy Award for *Boys' Town*, putting Judy Garland and Mickey Rooney through their paces in *Girl Crazy*, and directing Judy again in *Little Nellie Kelly* and *Presenting Lily Mars*. Taurog never made a great picture, but he rarely made a dull one.

We mentioned him once to a group of film buffs and got an astonished question: "You mean *he* got an Academy *Award?*" Yes, he did, for *Skippy* in the 1930–1931 season.

The picture, written by Joseph L. Mankiewicz, who was just getting started as a screen writer, was no marvel. The script was actually two stories in one. One plot involved the antics of two kids to save a dog from being destroyed in a pound. The second plot concerned Skippy's efforts to keep officials from closing Shantytown and depriving his friend Sooky of a home.

Taurog, a master at handling children anyway, brought out such endearing performances from his juvenile cast that one could not help liking the picture in spite of its shortcomings. This is probably why his Academy brethren thought Taurog did the best direction job of the year.

Charles Winninger and Judy Garland were in *Little Nelly Kelly,* based upon George M. Cohan's old stage success. Copyright 1940 by Metro-Goldwyn-Mayer.

Jackie Cooper and Robert Coogan (Jackie Coogan's brother) were in Taurog's *Skippy,* which the academy membership thought was the best directed picture of the 1930–1931 season. Copyright 1930 by Paramount-Publix Corporation.

**Jerry Lewis (left) was in Taurog's *Visit to a Small Planet*.
Copyright 1967 by Paramount Pictures Corporation.**

Also, it had the advantage of being based on a popular comic strip, Percy L. Crosby's *Skippy*. And, for once, the central human actor looked like the comic strip character. With his crushed hat and flowing tie and coat, Jackie Cooper looked just like the cartoon Skippy.

In the story, Sooky of Shantytown (Robert Coogan) must raise three dollars for a license to keep the pound from killing his dog. He and Skippy (Jackie Cooper) set out to raise the money. They fail, and the dog is destroyed. There is a weeping scene that made Cooper famous as a crybaby, and he had to weep in every picture for the next five years. His father (Willard Roberts) is so touched that he buys Skippy a bicycle. The boy trades it to Eloise (Mitzi Green) for her dog. He intends to give the dog to Sooky, but someone has already given the boy another dog and Skippy loses his bicycle for nothing.

Then a new crisis arises. Shantytown, considered a health menace, is to be burned. This will leave Sooky without a home, but Skippy persuades his father to have the place sprayed. This eliminates the health hazard and Shantytown is saved. Why didn't they do some slum clearance and rehabilitation? Ask Mankiewicz. He wrote the script.

After *Skippy*, Taurog went on to a long and profitable career. In his final years, he worked with Jerry Lewis. One of his Lewis films was *Visit to a Small Planet*.

Skippy (1931), produced by Jesse L. Lasky for Paramount Pictures Corporation release. Directed by Norman Taurog. Screenplay by Joseph L. Mankiewicz and Sam Mintz, from the comic strip by Percy L. Crosby. Principal cast members: Jackie Cooper, Robert Coogan, Mitzi Green, Jackie Searle, Willard Roberts.

Frank Borzage was the king of sentimentalists.
Copyright 1931 by Fox Film Corporation.

1931-1932

Frank Borzage for Bad Girl

After he scored his first big directorial success with *Humoresque* in 1920, Frank Borzage told an interviewer: "I intend to do stories of the people. I know the folks who go to movies are interested most of all in the problems, the joys and the sorrows of their own daily life, and I hope to bring to films the reflection of all this."

He certainly kept his word when he made *Bad Girl* eleven years later. The *New York Times* called the title "strangely unsuitable," but said the picture was blessed "with truth and simplicity." Actually, the title came from the best-selling book by Viña Delmar. Dorothy's (Sally Eilers) "badness" was getting pregnant before getting married. But Eddie (James Dunn) made an "honest woman" of her and the remainder of the book was an excellent description of the trials of a pregnant woman, told with more frankness than most books of the time.

Borzage casually dismissed all this and turned out a love story that—despite the different setting—was almost a continuation of *Seventh Heaven*. There are no villains and no melodrama. The plot deals with the strains of the first year of marriage, complicated by a coming baby. Both husband and wife assume—incorrectly—that the other does not want the child.

Dorothy is worried about the kind of doctor they can afford. She and Eddie talk it over. She speaks wistfully of Doctor Burgess, a famous specialist who caters only to the very wealthy. Eddie is determined to get the doctor for her. He begins working extra hours and even picks up some money boxing for ten dollars per bout.

When he has $350 saved, he approaches the doctor. He makes his pitch and promises to pay more as soon as he can earn it. The doctor, both touched and amused, agrees to deliver the baby. In a characterization that reminds us of Charles Farrell's role in *Seventh Heaven*, Eddie thinks he should say something complimentary to the kindly doctor. All he can think of to say is, "Gee, Doc, you got a swell dump here."

When the baby is born, the doctor marks the bill paid, and adds fifty dollars from his own pocket to start the child's bank account. The elated couple start home from the hospital with the baby. The taxi Eddie hires hits a bump. Eddie admonishes the driver to be more careful, for, after all, they have a passenger who may be a future president of the United States.

Sally Eilers, James Dunn, and Minna Gombell as Sally's wisecracking friend all came in for high critical praise. William A. Johnson, writing in *Motion Picture Herald*, said, "Honors go to Frank Borzage for a finely sustained balance of laughter and tears . . . with pictures like this, the hue of the fall box office grows rosier."

Other reviewers were impressed by Borzage's handling of dialogue in the picture, although the *New York Times* complained about the dialogue being slangy. Less pedantic reviews thought the slang added realism.

Borzage received his second Oscar for directing *Bad Girl*, and Edwin Burke got another for his adaption and dialogue. The film might have won the top picture award in a different year, but it had the misfortune to be pitted against *Grand Hotel*. Young love did not stand a chance against the combined might of Garbo, John and Lionel Barrymore, Wallace Beery, and Joan Crawford.

Some of Borzage's other films were: *They Had to See Paris* (1929) with Will Rogers, *A Farewell to Arms* (1933) with Gary Cooper and Helen Hayes, *Little Man What Now?* (1934) with Margaret Sullavan, and several Dick Powell-Ruby Keeler musicals.

***Bad Girl*, with Sally Eilers and James Dunn, brought Frank Borzage his second director's Oscar. Copyright 1931 by Fox Film Corporation.**

Bad Girl (1931), produced and released by Fox Film Corporation. Directed by Frank Borzage. Continuity and dialogue by Edwin Burke, from the novel by Viña Delmar. Photographed by Chester Lyons. Principal cast members: James Dunn, Sally Eilers, Minna Gombell, William Frawley, Frank Darien.

One of Frank Borzage's early talkies was *They Had to See Paris* with Fifi D'Orsay and Will Rogers. Copyright 1929 by Fox Film Corporation.

Gary Cooper and Helen Hayes were the lovers in Frank Borzage's version of *A Farewell to Arms.* Copyright 1932 by Paramount-Publix Corporation.

Frank Lloyd and his cameraman (right) discuss a scene with Isabel Jewell in 1918. Copyright 1918 by Fox Film Corporation.

1932-1933

Frank Lloyd
for Cavalcade

Cavalcade, the top Oscar picture for 1932–1933, was a totally British picture—an old-school-tie tribute to the glory of the empire, and God Bless the Queen. It was written by Noel Coward and starred that compleat Britisher, Clive Brook.

By rights, it should have had a British director. There were certainly plenty of them around, but the man chosen was a displaced Scotsman, Frank Lloyd (1889–1960). Although Scotland is part of the empire, there is a considerable difference in attitude between the two peoples. Lloyd got the assignment because of his Academy Award-winning direction of that earlier Hail Britannia film, *The Divine Lady*.

It was a good choice. Lloyd, working on a film quite different from his usual stories, did an outstanding job artistically and cinematically.

The film was revived not too long ago, and the program notes lauded its great success. Unfortunately, *Cavalcade*'s successes were all artistic. The academy gave it best film and best direction Oscars, and critics were lyrical. Since it touched upon the breakdown of social barriers, the liberals sang its praises as well. Financially, it flopped. William C. deMille, a liberal himself, commented on its failure at the box office with the observation that the public did not want literate film entertainment.

DeMille is a bit inaccurate in this observation. The record shows that the public will accept literate entertainment, *if* it is *entertainment*. So much of this literate stuff just isn't.

The trouble with *Cavalcade* is that it was one of those sprawling dynastic things in which the characters grow old and the audience grows tired. It covered English history, which the depression audiences of 1932–1933 were not particularly interested in anyway, from 1899 to 1933.

The film opens with the Marryot family preparing for its traditional New Year's toast at midnight, 31 December 1899. The usual joy is tempered because Robert (Clive Brook) is going off to the Boer War. He returns a hero and with Diana Wynyard's conjugal assistance, raises sons to carry on the traditions of the

Empire. They pass through the changes brought about by the death of Queen Victoria, the sinking of the Titanic, World War I, and the changing social values of the 1920s.

In the final years, they face the social shock of their son's desire to marry the daughter of their former maid.

The film closes with another New Year and Miss Wynyard's toast: "Let's couple the future of England with the past of England. The glorious victories and triumphs that are over, and the troubles that are over, too. Let's drink to our sons who made part of the pattern and to our hearts that went with them. Let's drink

Cavalcade, which won Frank Lloyd his second director's Oscar, was a beautiful picture that was poorly received by the public. Clive Brook and Diana Wynyard were the stars. Copyright 1933 by Fox Film Corporation.

Lloyd's most famous film, although by no means his best, was *Mutiny on the Bounty* with Charles Laughton as Captain Bligh. Copyright 1935 by Metro-Goldwyn-Mayer.

Children of Divorce, with Gary Cooper and Clara Bow, was one of Frank Lloyd's less happy efforts. Copyright 1927 by Famous Players-Lasky Corporation.

to the spirit of gallantry and courage . . . and let's drink to the hope that one day this country of ours will find dignity, greatness, and peace again."

And Clive Brook echoes her final words: "Dignity, greatness, peace."

Cavalcade was different from the usual Lloyd picture. This versatility may have been why the academy voted him the director's Oscar. Fox did not spare money and the production values were good, all of which helped.

Also in 1933, Lloyd made *Berkeley Square*, with Leslie Howard and Norma Shearer, and *Hoopla*, a flop, with Clara Bow in a remake of the role created by Dorothy Mackaill in *The Barker*. But he came back with a bang in 1935 after leaving Fox for MGM, where his first film was *Mutiny on the Bounty*, with Charles Laughton and Clark Gable. This was followed by such films as *Under Two Flags* (1936), *Maid of Salem* (1937), and *If I were King* (1938). After this there was a gradual decline until he made his final film, *The Last Command*, in 1955. He died in 1960 after a long career that he began as an actor and then actor-director for Universal in 1913. Although he slipped occasionally, as in *Children of Divorce* (1927), in the main, Frank Lloyd was a very entertaining director. That may not be a flattering statement to today's film critics, but those who enjoyed his pictures can appreciate what it means.

Cavalcade (1933), Fox Film Corporation release. Directed by Frank Lloyd. Screenplay by Reginald Berkeley, from the play by Noel Coward. Principal cast members: Clive Brook, Diana Wynyard, Herbert Mundin, Una O'Conner. Bonita Granville had a bit as a child.

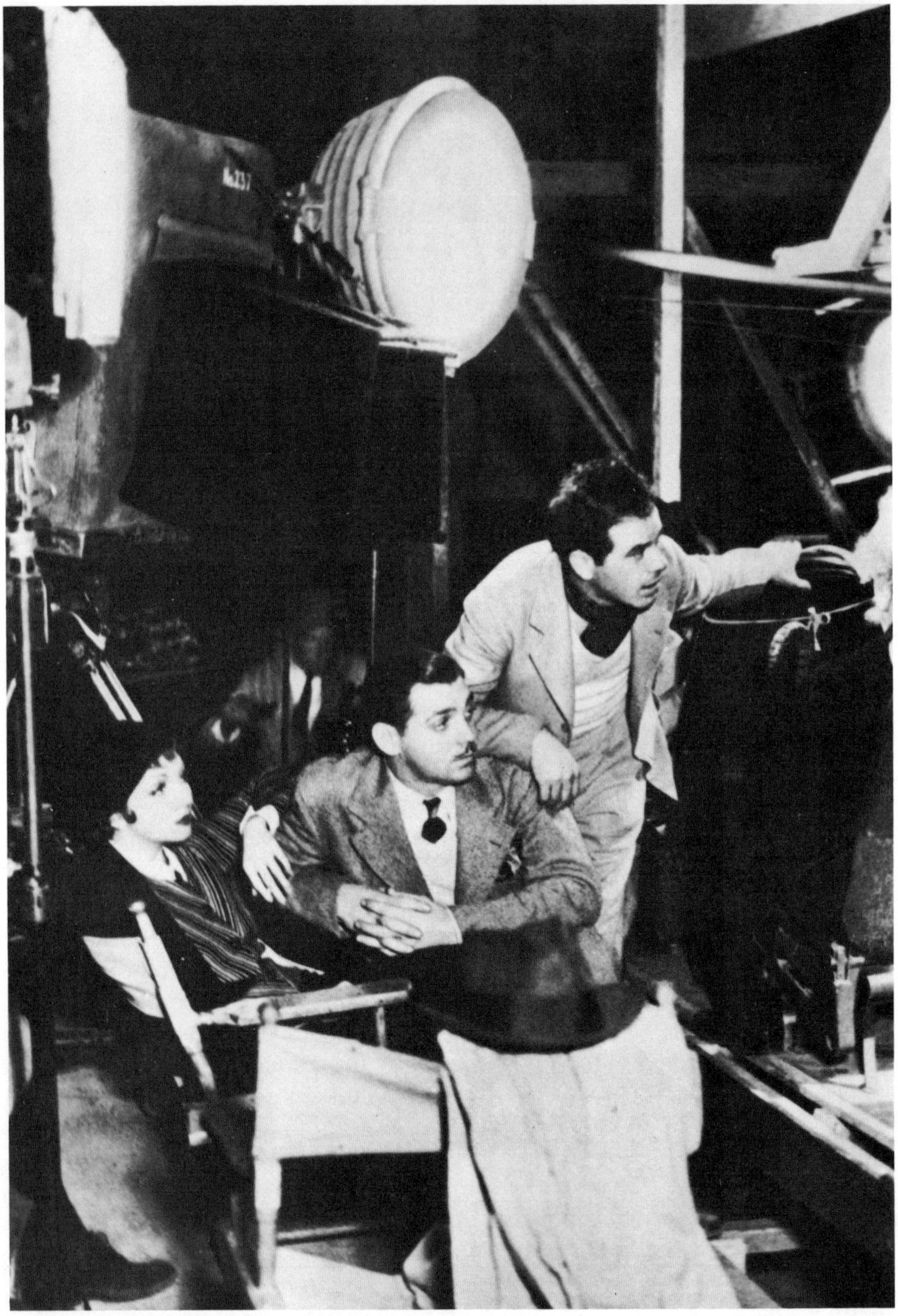

Frank Capra, right, sets up a scene for *It Happened One Night*, while stars Claudette Colbert and Clark Gable wait for the camera call. The film has become a comedy classic. Copyright 1934 by Columbia Pictures Corporation.

1934

Frank Capra for It Happened One Night

Frank Capra was born in Palermo, Italy, in 1898 and came to the United States in 1901. His father was a fruit picker. There was nothing in the family background to indicate a theatrical future for young Frank. He wanted to be an engineer and whacked a banjo in an orchestra to pay his way through the California Institute of Technology. The class prophecy predicted that the Army would refuse to take him as a general and that he would join Mack Sennett as a Keystone Kop.

There were no jobs for chemical engineers when Frank graduated. He bummed around and became a book salesman until 1924. At this time, an old actor, Walter Montague, had an idea of making one-reel films based upon famous poems. The first was to be Rudyard Kipling's *Fultah Fisher's Boarding House*. Capra read about this in the newspaper and went to see Montague about selling him some books. Montague was in San Francisco. Capra introduced himself as from Los Angeles.

Montague brightened. "From Hollywood?" he asked eagerly.

"Oh, yes," Capra replied. His book selling experience had taught him to always agree with a prospective customer.

"You are heaven sent!" Montague cried. "I need a director. I can pay $75 a week."

"I'll take it," Capra replied. Judging by the pictures he had seen, he thought anyone could direct one.

They imported a cameraman from Hollywood. Capra recruited some amateur actors, and, with the cameraman's help, shot the film for $1,700. Montague sold it to Pathe for $3,500, almost a 100 per cent profit.

"Movie making is a gold mine," Capra told himself. "I had better learn something about it." He turned down Montague's offer to make another one-reeler, and headed for Hollywood. He got a job as prop man and then as a gagman for Hal Roach. Later Capra switched to Mack Sennett, almost making the class prophecy come true.

Capra worked as a gagman for Sennett and then became a director, moving with comedian Harry Langdon to First National where he scored a huge success as director of *The Strong Man* (1926). Later Langdon decided he wanted to be his own director and fired Capra, who went back to Mack Sennett until he was hired by Harry Cohn at Columbia to make B pictures.

Capra scored with two early talkies for Cohn, *Platinum Blonde* (1931), with Jean Harlow, who was fresh from Howard Hughes' *Hell's Angels*. An even bigger success was *Lady for a Day* (1933), a Damon Runyon fable about gamblers who pass off an old appleseller (May Robson) as a lady in high society to get her daughter married into a rich, snobbish family.

Capra followed this success with *It Happened One Night* (1934), with Claudette Colbert and Clark Gable. Again he achieved a financial and critical success. The film received a number of Academy Award nominations, but no one gave Capra much chance to receive the director's award. The film was a comedy

Capra made an excursion into oriental philosophy with *Lost Horizon* (1937). This scene shows Sam Jaffe, Ronald Colman, Thomas Mitchell, Isabel Jewell, and Edward Everett Horton. Copyright 1937 by Columbia Pictures Corporation.

Jean Harlow and Robert Williams were in Capra's *Platinum Blonde*. Williams got exceptional reviews, but died soon after, ending what appeared to be a sure climb to stardom. Copyright 1931 by Columbia Pictures Corporation.

and Capra's chances would have been better in earlier years when the academy picked two best directors—one for drama and one for comedy. This separation was eliminated after the first awards.

So, when Capra started another comedy, he was apparently wiped out of the 1934 awards consideration. This was especially true since the story involved a runaway heiress and a poor newspaperman—as trite a situation as could be found on stage or screen.

His female star was Claudette Colbert, who was personable enough, but had not yet set the screen on fire. His male star was Clark Gable, another still to make his mark, although he was coming up fast. The rumor around film row was that Clark was shipped off to Poverty Row and the terrible-mannered Mr. Cohn as punishment for getting out of hand on his home MGM lot. He was then a long way from becoming "The King."

Out of this unlikely material, Frank Capra fashioned *It Happened One Night*, which swept the awards for best picture, best actor and actress, and best director. This was the first time that had happened. For once, the awards were richly deserved by all concerned. Anyone who could take a trite runaway-heiress story and turn it into a classic comedy that would still have critics nodding approval forty-five years later must be a genius, although a share of the glory should go to his writer, another man of comic genius, Robert Riskin.

The script was based on the magazine story *Night Bus* by Samuel Hopkins Adams, who would later contribute the original story for Judy Garland's *The Harvey Girls*. As the film opens, heiress Ellen Andrews (Colbert) is in revolt against her father (Walter Connolly). He locks her in a yacht stateroom to prevent her from marrying a lounge lizard, as playboys were called in those long-ago days. Ellen escapes and starts to travel to New York by bus to marry her boyfriend. Her bag and money are stolen, throwing her on the mercy of an out-of-work newspaper reporter, Peter Warne (Gable).

The bus is wrecked in an almost Sennett-like sequence, and then Ellen and Peter are on their own, hitchhiking to New York. On the way they fall in love. Ellen does not realize this until she is walking up the aisle to marry her playboy. Then she flees back to Gable.

In outline, this is a thousand-times-told tale, but what Capra does with it is unique. He laughs at sex and everything else. Ernst Lubitsch had been doing this in his continental manner, but Capra did it in an American manner that made his audiences understand, laugh, and wish they were in Gable's place.

Some of the individual scenes have become famous. There is the one where Gable is giving Colbert lessons in how to hitchhike. After he has more than eighty failures with different techniques, she shows him how: She raises her skirt to display a shapely leg, and the first car skids to a screeching halt. Mack Sennett had used essentially the same gag many times, but the interplay between Gable and Colbert—all due to Capra's direction—turned the burlesque gag into a comedy triumph.

Another famous scene is the motel sequence. Colbert was rather prudish, so Gable rigged up a curtain between their beds. He called this barrier the "walls of Jericho." In the Bible, Joshua fought the battle of Jericho and the walls came tumbling down. Eventually, these walls tumbled as well.

Scenes that 1934 audiences found delightfully risqué are laughably innocent according to today's license, but *It Happened One Night* was daring for its day. Some liberal reviewers tried to find a social undercurrent because the rich woman learns to prefer the simple life of the poor, but the public found only fun. Frank Capra deserved this first Oscar more than the other two he got. It takes great direction to turn what he had to work with into a romantic comedy classic.

It Happened One Night (1934), produced by Harry Cohn for Columbia Pictures Corporation release. Directed by Frank Capra. Screenplay by Robert Riskin, from the short story *Night Bus* by Samuel Hopkins Adams. Principal cast members: Claudette Colbert, Clark Gable, Walter Connolly, Alan Hale, Roscoe Karns.

The blanket between Claudette Colbert and Clark Gable will come tumbling down before *It Happened One Night* reaches the final reel. This classic film won the director's Oscar for Frank Capra, best actor and actress awards for Colbert and Gable, and also took best picture honors. Copyright 1934 by Columbia Pictures Corporation.

John Ford, a four-time Oscar winner, was a Hollywood legend. Copyright 1929 by Fox Film Corporation.

1935

John Ford
for The Informer

John Ford (1895–1973) was the son of Irish immigrants who settled in Maine, where he and his brother Francis were born. The family name was O'Fearna, which became Feeney after the family got to America. John never deserted his Irish background, and some of his best pictures were deeply rooted in the *auld sod.*

His older brother, Francis, became an actor under the name of Francis Ford. While working for Thomas H. Ince in 1911, when stage roles were hard to find, Francis met Grace Cunard, who had a talent for writing as well as acting. They teamed up professionally and moved to Universal in late 1912 as a writer-director-actor-actress team. Grace wrote the scripts, Francis directed, and both played leads.

In 1913, John, then eighteen, came west to join his brother in the picture business. He worked as a prop boy and a utility actor. In one interview, he told a fanciful story of being fired by Francis from his first film because he made the sign of the cross before taking a dangerous leap off a bridge in one scene.

It's a nice story, but John was not fired from his first acting job and thereby forced to become a director or starve. He played quite a number of parts in the Ford-Cunard two-reelers. His face can be clearly seen in the stills. Also, he had the second male lead after Francis in the 1915 two-reeler, *Three Bad Men and a Girl.*

He just did not have the looks to be a matinee idol, and, in 1917, he became a director after assisting Francis on several films. He made pictures on an assembly-line basis for Universal and then for Fox before he got his first critical notices for *The Iron Horse,* a story of the building of the transcontinental railroad, in 1924.

He made the transition to talkies with ease, doing a surprisingly good job on *Arrowsmith* (1931), with Ronald Colman as the young doctor. This was followed by some popular, if not substantial, Will Rogers vehicles. Then, in 1935, after numerous turndowns, he finally got RKO to let him make *The Informer,* a grim, downbeat story of a conscience-stricken drunkard who betrays a comrade during the Irish revolt.

The film was rooted in Ford's Irish heritage and he handled it as a labor of love, although he was cramped by a minimum budget.

The film, based on Liam O'Flaherty's novel, follows the unities of classic drama. It takes place in a single night within a three-block section of Dublin, Ireland, in 1921.

As the film opens, Gypo Nolan (Victor McLaglen) sees a poster offering a reward of twenty pounds for information on his fugitive friend (Wallace Ford). Gypo is in love with a prostitute (Margot Grahame) and wants to escape with her to America. The temptation is too great. He goes to military headquarters and informs on his friend, who is killed resisting the arrest.

Gypo gets his money and heads for a saloon to get liquor to drown his already nagging conscience. His suspicious fellow-revolutionists put him on trial. Drunk and despairing, answering the accusations flung at him, he shouts, "I didn't know what I was doing!"

Breaking away, he is shot from ambush. He staggers into a church where he finds his dead friend's mother (Una O'Conner) praying for her son's soul. Crying, he begs her forgiveness. Then, crying out to the dead man's spirit, "Frankie, your mother forgives me!" he dies.

The low key, foggy photography by Joe August exactly fitted the mood of the film, and the splendid acting by McLaglen, supported by Irishman Ford's love and sympathy for the subject, worked together to make a truly outstanding film. *The Informer* and *What Price Glory?* are the two high spots in McLaglen's career.

Except for the overly maudlin ending, *The Informer* was a powerful psychological picture of the disintegration of a man's personality. This has been shown more popularly but never better by any film, actor, or director. The story and direction kept to a narrow dramatic line. There were no blind alleys, no confusing subplots. It was simply the story of Gypo Noland's psychological collapse. Dudley Nichols wrote a script that was a model for storytellers.

The Iron Horse **brought Ford his first critical acclaim. George O'Brien, J. Farrell MacDonald, and Madge Bellamy were in the cast. Copyright 1924 by Fox Film Corporation.**

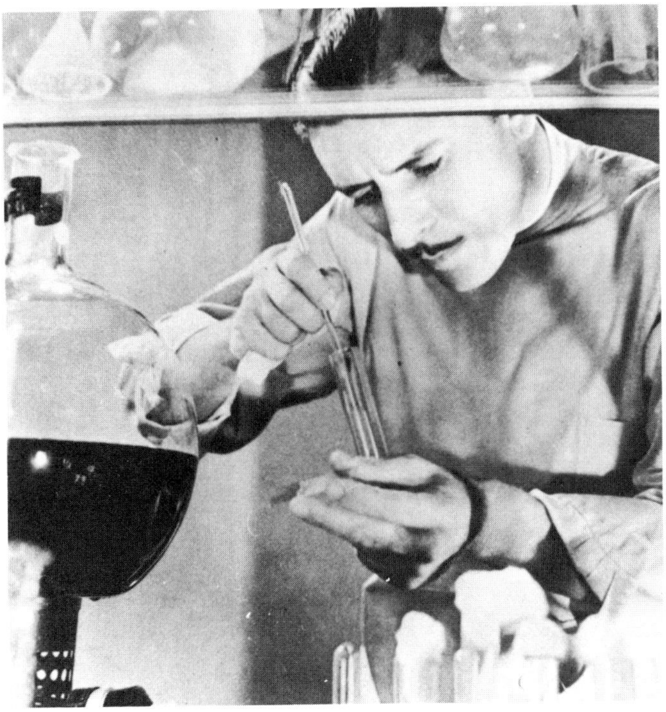

Arrowsmith, with Ronald Colman in the Sinclair Lewis story, was one of John Ford's early talkie successes. Copyright 1931 by Samuel Goldwyn Productions.

Margot Grahame finds Victor McLaglen trying to drown his conscience in wine in this scene from *The Informer.* Copyright 1935 by RKO-Radio Pictures, Incorporated.

A superior film, it was unfortunately bucking the trend to screwball comedies and was not a financial success. The Academy membership thought enough of it to give acting honors to McLaglen and the director's Oscar to Ford, but decided to give the best picture nod to the highly popular, but less artistic, *Mutiny on the Bounty,* directed by Frank Lloyd.

The Informer (1935), released by RKO-Radio Pictures Incorporated. Directed by John Ford. Screenplay by Dudley Nichols, from the novel by Liam O'Flaherty. Photographed by Joe August. Principal cast members: Victor McLaglen, Margot Grahame, Una O'Conner, Wallace Ford.

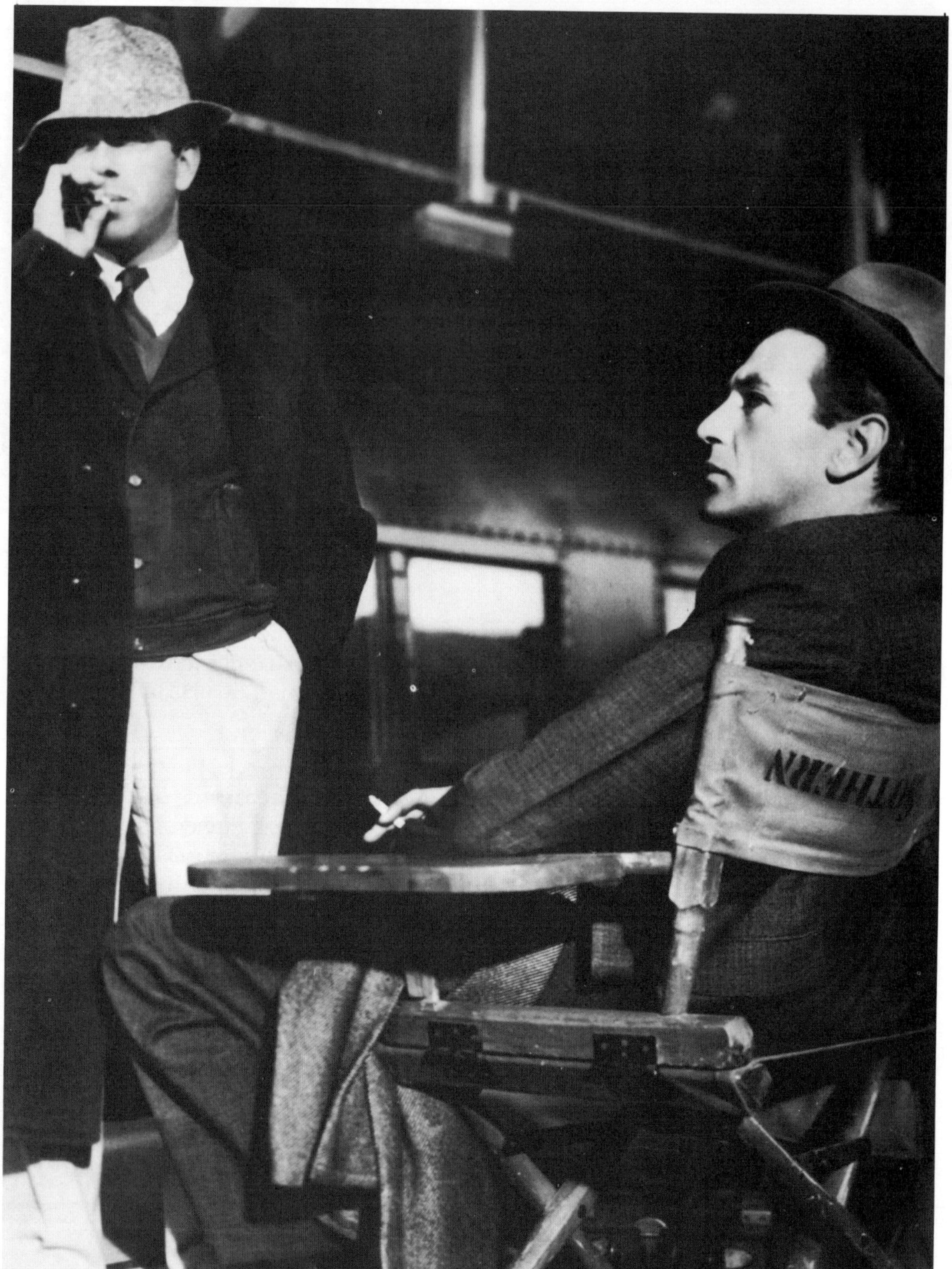

Frank Capra with Gary Cooper on the set of *Mr. Deeds Goes to Town.* Copyright 1936 by Columbia Pictures Corporation.

1936

Frank Capra
for Mr. Deeds Goes to Town

By 1934, the Academy Awards were beginning to attract more public attention, but they were still far from the box office hit they later became. At this time, they were still more important to Hollywood people than to the general public.

Frank Capra has admitted that he wanted one badly. His ambition to be acclaimed the best director of the year by his peers seemed presumptuous in a man only a few years removed from writing gags for Mack Sennett. He had made some good pictures. *Long Pants* (1926), his last picture at First National with Harry Langdon, *Platinum Blonde* (1931), the better than average adventure film, *Dirigible* (1931), and *Lady for a Day* (1933) were among them.

Then came his Academy Award hit, *It Happened One Night* (1934). His friends were happy for Frank, but none dreamed that he would make Academy Awards almost a habit.

After *It Happened One Night* Capra decided that he should put a bit of social significance into his films. Fortunately for him, Columbia Pictures, and the public, Capra's newly found regard for the common man did not obscure his sense of humor. The result was *Mr. Deeds Goes to Town*, which earned Capra his second director's Oscar.

Mr. Deeds is based upon a ridiculous premise—that Longfellow Deeds (Gary Cooper), a poor man who writes greeting card verse to earn his living, would rather stay home and play his tuba than go to New York and collect a $20 million inheritance. However, pressure forces Deeds (Gary Cooper) to go to New York. He is established in his dead uncle's mansion and is immediately besieged by a legion of people wanting part of his money. One request is from an opera group that needs $100,000 to pay off a deficit. Deeds tells them that they probably have been putting on the wrong kind of show.

Among the parasites who surround Deeds is Babe Bennett (Jean Arthur), a newspaper woman assigned to keep Deeds on the front page. She comes to admire his small-town qualities and love blossoms between them. Then Deeds learns that he has been her newspaper assignment. Embittered, he intends to return to Mandrake Falls to play his tuba.

At this point, a bitter farmer (John Wray) bursts in on Deeds and threatens to shoot him. When the farmer breaks down, Deeds invites him to lunch and listens to the man's problems. Deeds then decides to spend his fortune buying land for dispossessed, starving people like this farmer.

Deeds' lawyers are horrified, for they are trying to cover up a half-million dollar embezzlement made from the estate. To stop the money giveaway, they accuse Deeds of being crazy. A court hearing is set to determine Deed's sanity. Things look bad for the hero and his reinstated girlfriend, Babe. Two nice old ladies (Margaret Seddon and Margaret McWade) make a strong impression on the court when they testify that Deeds is "pixilated." Deeds is saved when his lawyer asks the witnesses if they know any other pixilated people. The ladies reply, "Oh, everyone but us!"

So Deeds is declared sane, gets the girl, and, presumably, he gives money away happily ever after.

The picture was a hit. Capra got his second Oscar for direction, but, looking at it today, it is hard to see why. The plot was ridiculous, the story line was thin, and the message was weak. The gags, such as Deeds sliding down a bannister, were good and fit the situation. But, all in all, the best that can be said for *Mr. Deeds Goes to Town* is that the public in 1936 thought it great fun.

Long Pants **starred Harry Langdon with Phyllis Bonner.**
Copyright 1927 by First National Pictures.

Dirigible with Fay Wray, Ralph Graves and Jack Holt was one of the bread-and-butter films Capra directed for Harry Cohn. Copyright 1931 by Columbia Pictures Corporation.

Gary Cooper as Longfellow Deeds is somewhat suspicious of his newly acquired butler (Raymond Walburn) in *Mr. Deeds Goes to Town*, the film that earned Frank Capra his second director's Oscar. Copyright renewed 1974 by Columbia Pictures Industries, Inc.

Mr. Deeds Goes to Town (1936), Produced by Harry Cohn for Columbia Pictures Corporation release. Directed by Frank Capra. Screenplay by Robert Riskin, from the story by Frank Budington Kelland. Principal cast members: Gary Cooper, Jean Arthur, John Wray.

Leo McCarey received the Academy Award for best achievement in directing twice. His sense of comedy was second to none. Copyright 1928 by Hal Roach Studios.

1937

Leo McCarey for The Awful Truth

"Uncle Tom" McCarey was a fight promoter in Los Angeles, California, at the turn of the century. One of the requirements for a fight promoter in those days was the ability to lick any boxer, manager, or irate spectator who took exception to any of the sometimes peculiar dealings that were part of the fight game in those long-ago days.

That meant that Uncle Tom was tough. So, when he told his son Leo to forget any other ideas he might have and go to law school, young Leo knew better than to argue. Uncle Tom wanted a lawyer in the family so he could get out of jail free if the need arose. Leo dutifully graduated from law school and joined a San Francisco law firm. He lost his first case in fifteen minutes and his position with the law firm in three more.

Next, Leo tried running his own law office. This venture ended when a burly client, enraged when Leo lost his case, chased the lawyer down the street. At least, this is Leo's account of why he gave up the law for motion pictures.

In 1919 or 1920, David Butler, an actor of sorts who later turned a director, became a drinking buddy of Leo's. Purely in self defense, so that Leo could afford to buy an occasional round instead of always sponging off Dave, Butler introduced McCarey to Tod Browning. Browning, who later gained fame as the director of Lon Chaney thrillers and Bela Lugosi's *Dracula*, was just hitting his stride at Universal.

Browning had nothing for a man who admitted he could not do anything. But, to shut Butler up, Browning offered McCarey the only opening he had. The script girl had just quit, and Leo became the first male script girl.

All in all, he did well enough to be promoted to assistant director. He worked with Browning on *The Virgin of Stamboul* (1920) with Priscilla Dean and *Outside the Law* (1921), in which Lon Chaney, in a dual role of a Chinese and a gangster, murdered himself.

After this, Leo talked himself into a director's slot on *Society Secrets* (1921) with Eva Novak. All that is known about this picture is that it sent McCarey back to assistant directing; he did not rise from there for five years.

Then Hal Roach, the comedy maker, took him on as a gagman. He did well and eventually became production head for Roach. He is credited with being the genius who brought Stan Laurel and Oliver Hardy together.

McCarey quit Roach in 1929, claiming that Hal was too healthy and he could never hope to become president of the firm. He then blarneyed Joseph P. Kennedy, who was trying to straighten out a messy situation at Pathé-RKO, into letting him direct. The result was *The Sophomore* (1929) with Eddie Quillan, a film that seems to owe a lot to Harold Lloyd's *The Freshman*.

The Sophomore was a hit, and Leo moved into higher movie-society. He directed Jack Oakie and Jeanette MacDonald in *Let's Go Native* (1930), Eddie Cantor in *The Kid from Spain* (1933), Mae West in *Belle of the Nineties* (1934), Charles Laughton giving a marvelous performance in *Ruggles of Red Gap* (1935), and Harold Lloyd in *The Milky Way* (1936).

McCarey, as production head with Hal Roach, is credited with teaming Laurel and Hardy. Here Stan and Ollie cut up in the two-reeler *Putting Pants on Phillip*. Copyright 1927 by Hal Roach Studios.

Eddie Quillan was a fumbling football rookie in *The Sophomore,* the second feature film McCarey directed. Copyright 1929 by Pathé Pictures.

Then, after all those years with comedy, McCarey decided he wanted to make a statement. So he directed *Make Way for Tomorrow,* a movie about the cruelty of children to their parents. Crushed by its failure, McCarey said, "If they only want Hal Roach, that's what I'll give them!"

He dusted off an old stage bedroom farce which Ina Claire had filmed for Pathé in 1929, *The Awful Truth.* Columbia gave him Irene Dunne and Cary Grant. He rushed it through and went to Europe to drown his sorrow over the failure of *Make Way for Tomorrow.* Then he got a telegram asking him to come back to pick up his Oscar. He thought that *Make Way* had at last been recognized, but, to his great surprise, *The Awful Truth* took the directorial prize for 1937.

The only possible explanation for this is that the academy membership felt like laughing that year. *The Awful Truth* does not meet any of the basic criteria for a great motion picture. It is devoid of social significance. It has no obscure symbolism. It dispenses with character development. It breaks no new ground in cinematic techniques. All the picture did was make people laugh.

The story reaches the acme of triteness. Hiding men in bedrooms when new beaus showed up had been presented thousands of times on stage and screen. Someone counted and found that Mack Sennett alone had used the gimmick at least 100 times. But, whatever its flaws, among McCarey, Dunne, and Grant, bedroom farce became a triumph of romantic, slightly screwball comedy.

The Awful Truth begins when Jerry Warriner (Cary Grant) pretends to take a trip to Florida so he can actually stay in New York for a few days on the town without Lucy, his wife (Irene Dunne). When he returns home, in comes Lucy with a handsome music teacher (Alexander D'Arcy). Both Jerry and Lucy present good explanations, but each refuses to believe the other. They divorce, and Lucy gets custody of the dog, Mr. Smith, but Jerry gets visiting rights to see the dog.

They are constantly thrown in each other's way. When Jerry goes to Lucy's home to exercise his visiting rights with the dog, Armand, the music teacher, is there. Knowing Jerry is still jealous of him, Lucy makes Armand hide in the bedroom. Then Lucy's other boy friend (Ralph Bellamy) arrives, and Lucy shoves Jerry into the bedroom. All three men are angry at Lucy.

Then Lucy crashes an engagement party for Jerry and a socialite who has trapped him. She tricks Jerry into taking her home, and they end up in a mountain cabin and back in each other's arms.

Reviewers united in calling it the funniest comedy of the year. The academy, while judging *The Life of Emile Zola* the best picture, thought Leo the best director.

The Awful Truth (1937), produced by Harry Cohn for Columbia Pictures Corporation release. Directed by Leo McCarey. Screenplay by Viña Delmar. Principal cast members: Cary Grant, Irene Dunne, Alexander D'Arcy, Ralph Bellamy.

Irene Dunne and Cary Grant were in *The Awful Truth,* a bedroom farce that brought McCarey his first Oscar for direction. Copyright 1937 by Columbia Pictures Corporation.

Frank Capra received his third Oscar in 1938 for *You Can't Take It with You.* Copyright 1938 by Columbia Pictures Corporation.

1938

Frank Capra for You Can't Take it With You

The word got around that Frank Capra's movies had a liberal streak. This put the predominantly liberal reviews strongly on his side. Actually, a close review of Capra's films doesn't really show much liberalism. There was definitely a "for-the-little-man" attitude in his pictures, starting with that epitome of the down-trodden Harry Langdon, but Harry, Longfellow Deeds, and John Doe were too eccentric to bring about any real social reform. Most ridiculous of all, there was even an attempt in some quarters to find liberalism in *It Happened One Night*. If this picture is liberalism, then so is *Cinderella*.

Capra has given the impression that he was trying to get a message into his films. Fortunately for him and for those of us who went to the movies in the 1930s, Capra's messages got lost in the fun and laughter. There is no better way to present messages on the screen.

We never knew we were supposed to be propagandized until we read about it years later in some book analyzing the screen.

Actually, it was difficult to determine what Capra's message was. In one of his best films, *You Can't Take It with You*, the message appears to be anarchy. Any other producer at the time would have been stoned out of Hollywood for such a proposition, but the heroine was pretty and the hero—in the Capra tradition—was not so smart, and everybody had a lot of fun.

Actually, *You Can't Take It with You* is more like a film for the sixties and seventies than the thirties. It preached against paying taxes and for everyone doing just what he or she chose. Grandpa Vanderhof's attitude toward the Internal Revenue Service could have been taken right off today's newspaper front page stories about tax revolts.

The difference was that Capra never dwelt on the sordid, cruel side of the social structure. He showed us the funny side, making himself and Columbia Pictures rich in the process.

You Can't Take It with You takes us into the home of Grandpa Vanderhof (Lionel Barrymore). Grandpa's philosophy is summed up when he asks Boris

(Mischa Auer) how granddaughter Essie (Ann Miller) is doing with her ballet lessons. Boris answers honestly, "She stinks." Grandpa nods pleasantly and replies, "As long as she enjoys it."

Just as Essie devotes herself to ballet, so each member of the family does his or her own thing. Grandpa does not pay taxes, for he does not believe in them. His daughter Penny (Spring Byington) writes plays because a typewriter was delivered by mistake; she uses a sleepy kitten for a paperweight as she adds page after page to the growing pile of manuscript.

There are several eccentric hangers-on in addition to ballet master Boris. Mr. Poppins (Donald Meek) invents things. Penny's husband (Samuel S. Hinds) manufactures fireworks in the basement. Dub Taylor plays the xylophone and Halliwell Hobbes is an iceman who came to make a delivery and just stayed. Alice, Vanderhof's other granddaughter (Jean Arthur), is the only normal member of the odd family.

Alice has fallen in love with Tony Kirby (James Stewart). Tony brings his Wall Street-broker father (Edward Arnold) and his mother (Esther Forbes) to meet Alice's family. They are stunned to find the Vanderhof family's living room in chaos with everyone carrying on with his or her individual interest. To add to the Kirbys' confusion, Grandpa tries to convince Kirby that his money-making life is a crime against human nature.

Alice is embarrassed by her family. For a while, it appears that the romance will falter. Then Papa, by mistake, explodes the fireworks in the basement, and the police take them all to jail. But Kirby badly needs some property Grandpa owns. He gets the property, the complications are smoothed out, and Kirby acknowledges that Grandpa may have the right idea after all. The film closes with Kirby joining in the madcap antics of the family. Kirby's conversion seemed

Esther Forbes, James Stewart, Jean Arthur, and Edward Arnold in *You Can't Take It with You.* Copyright 1938 by Columbia Pictures Corporation.

Mr. Smith Goes to Washington was a political satire with Jean Arthur and James Stewart. Copyright 1939 by Columbia Pictures Corporation.

***Riding High* (1950) was a remake of Capra's successful *Broadway Bill* (1934), but it failed to score the second time around. Bing Crosby, Clarence Muse, and Colleen Gray were in the cast. Copyright 1949 by Paramount Pictures Corporation.**

rather false, but the picture was such great fun that the audience was willing to overlook a false note here and there.

Capra continued to be popular for the rest of the 1930s with films like *Mr. Smith Goes to Washington* (1939), and *Meet John Doe* (1941). During World War II, Capra made documentaries for the United States government. After the war, his films went into a decline. Even when he tried to remake an old success like *Broadway Bill* (1934), retitled *Riding High* (1950) and starring Bing Crosby, Capra could not regain his old magic.

You Can't Take It with You (1938), produced by Frank Capra for Columbia Pictures Corporation release. Directed by Frank Capra. Screenplay by Robert Riskin, from the play by George S. Kaufman and Moss Hart. Photographed by Joseph Walker. Principal cast members: James Stewart, Jean Arthur, Lionel Barrymore, Ann Miller, Mischa Auer, Spring Byington, Donald Meek, Samuel S. Hinds.

Victor Fleming directed two all-time classic films, *Gone with the Wind* and *The Wizard of Oz*. Copyright 1927 by Paramount Pictures Corporation.

1939

Victor Fleming for Gone with the Wind

Academy Awards are often controversial. But the award of the 1939 Oscar for direction to Victor Fleming (1883–1949) is probably the most questionable of them all. It is not a question of the film's direction deserving an Oscar, but a question of who *was* the real director of this famous film?

George Cukor started it and was in on the planning for two years. Then, two weeks after actual shooting started, Cukor was fired by the dictatorial producer David O. Selznick. He was replaced by Victor Fleming.

Selznick never gave a reason for firing Cukor. There has been a lot of speculation. One claim is that the star, Clark Gable, demanded Cukor's dismissal because the director was more interested in Vivien Leigh than in Gable. Another, and more credible, claim is that Cukor was proving too independent and Selznick, a true ego-maniac, intended to be the director in fact, if not in name.

In time, even Fleming could no longer stomach Selznick's continual interference. He became "sick." Sam Wood was brought in to take over. Fleming came back in two weeks. Whispers claimed that Selznick only took him back because Gable refused to continue unless Fleming, an old drinking buddy, was restored. In any event, Sam Wood was kept on to shoot with a second unit. William Cameron Menzies, the production designer, also shot some scenes.

So among Selznick, Fleming, Wood, Cukor, and Menzies, who did direct *Gone with the Wind*? The best authorities seem to feel that Fleming only shot between 40 and 50 per cent of the film. The rest was directed by others.

Fleming believed it was his picture. He objected violently, threatening court action, when Selznick wanted to give screen credit to Cukor and Wood. Selznick further infuriated Fleming by publicly bad-mouthing the director's contributions. According to the producer, Fleming merely carried out the orders of that supreme genius David O. Selznick.

This made Fleming so angry that he refused to attend the gala premiere of the picture in Atlanta, Georgia. His anger had not diminished when the Academy Awards were handed out. He was not at the banquet to receive his award.

There is little point in summarizing the plot of a picture as widely shown as *Gone with the Wind*. It is, basically, the story of the Civil War's effect upon a self-centered woman, Scarlett O'Hara. The casting was pure genius. The novel was a publishing phenomenon and one of the most widely read novels of modern times. Because of this, the characters were fixed in a multitude of minds. If the cast had not been exactly what the public expected, the film could have failed. Vivien Leigh and Clark Gable *were* Scarlett and Rhett Butler. The rest of the cast, including the minor characters, were equally matched with what the readers of Margaret Mitchell's book expected.

Victor Fleming, as the director of record, is the only one who has failed to receive the public and critical acclaim that direction of such a classic should bring. Most people seem to have accepted Selznick's claim that he did it all. There is no denying that Selznick's stamp is on every frame, but, when he tried to carry all the load in other films, he did not prove to be the genius of geniuses he fancied himself. We can see this in *A Farewell to Arms* (1957), *Portrait of Jenny* (1949), and *Duel in the Sun* (1946).

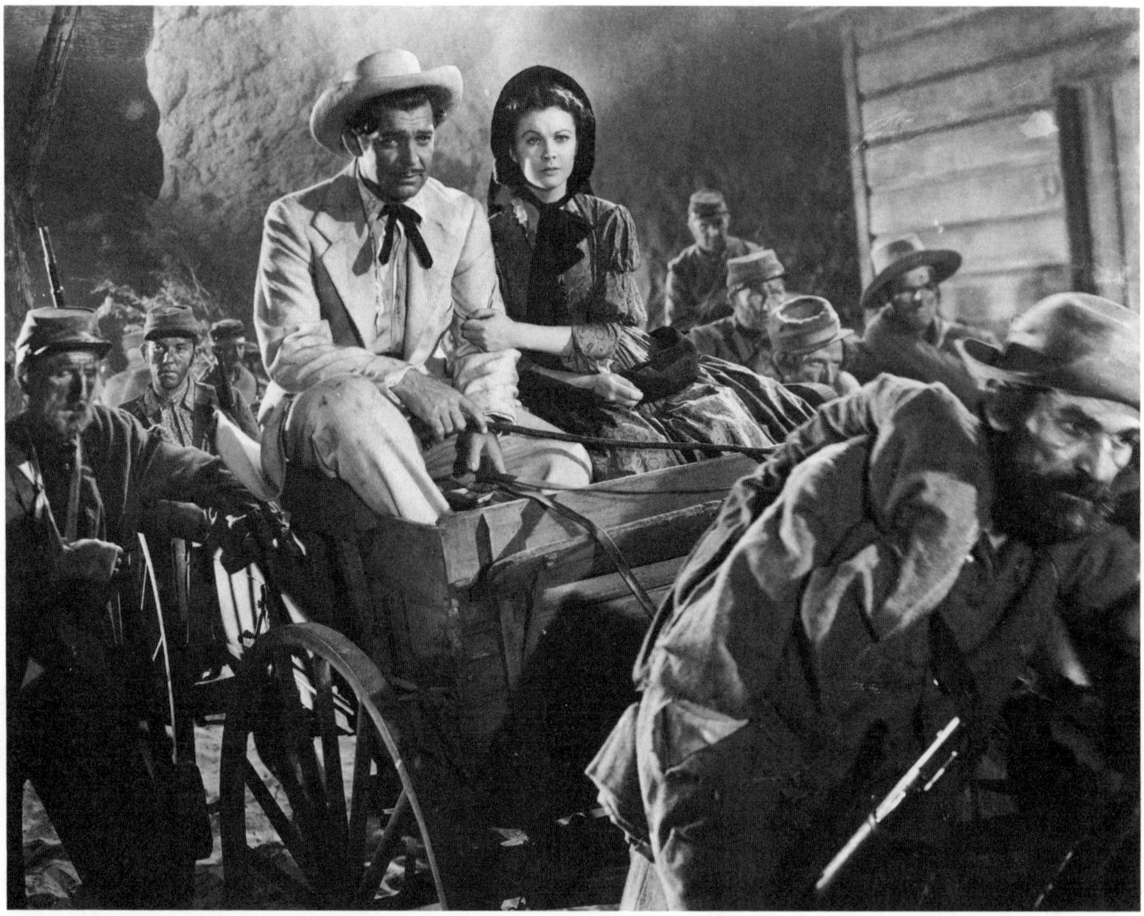

Clark Gable and Vivien Leigh flee from Atlanta in the historic film *Gone with the Wind*. Copyright 1939 by Metro-Goldwyn-Mayer.

The Mollycoddle **(1921), with Douglas Fairbanks, Sr., and Ruth Rennick, was Victor Fleming's second directorial assignment. Copyright 1921 by United Artists Corporation.**

Fleming's contributions to *Gone with the Wind* were certainly more substantial than he is credited for. When his supporters point out that he also made the classic *The Wizard of Oz*, this is dismissed with an airy, "Oh, that was due to Arthur Freed." Arthur Freed—song writer turned producer—is on record as saying that he never interfered with his directors. The fact is that Fleming was a far better director than most of the Hollywood variety.

He was born in 1883 in Pasadena, California, and became a Biograph cameraman. World War I saw him an officer in the United States Army Signal Corps and a member of President Woodrow Wilson's peace delegation to Europe in 1918. Apparently, he went along to oversee the Signal Corps movies of the event.

He returned to Hollywood in late 1919 as a cameraman for Douglas Fairbanks, Sr. In 1920, Fairbanks moved Fleming up to direct *When the Clouds Roll By* and, in 1921, *The Mollycoddle*. Fleming impressed Jesse L. Lasky, who invited the new director to Paramount. Fleming began with Realart, the Paramount B unit, on films for Agnes Ayres and Alice Brady before moving to the top with Richard Dix in *To the Last Man* (1923). He received good critical notices for his 1925 version of Joseph Conrad's *Lord Jim*, and then handled (that is the correct word for it) Clara Bow in *Mantrap* (1926).

Mantrap, the story of a golddigging manicurist, was Clara Bow's first unqualified success, and she became Fleming's girl friend. It was a romance of short duration. Clara said in an interview that she learned a lot from Fleming, but "he was too old for Little Clara." Fleming also directed Clara in *Hula* (1927).

Through the years, we find high critical praise for his *The Rough Riders* (1927) with Charles Farrell and Mary Astor, and *The Virginian* (1929), his and Gary Cooper's first all-talkie. Then we have *Red Dust* (1932) with Clark Gable and Jean Harlow, *Treasure Island* (1934) with Wallace Beery and Jackie Cooper, *Reckless* (1935) with Jean Harlow, *Captains Courageous* (1937) with Spencer Tracy, *Test Pilot* with Gable and Tracy, and then the classic *The Wizard of Oz*. That steady succession of hits is a record that few directors can match.

But fame and fortune ran out for Fleming after *Gone with the Wind*. His career went downhill with *Dr. Jekyll and Mr. Hyde* (1941), *Tortilla Flat* (1942), *A Guy Named Joe* (1943), *Adventure* (1946), and ended with an absolute failure, Ingrid Bergman in *Joan of Arc* (1948).

Gone with the Wind (1939), produced by David O. Selznick for Metro-Goldwyn-Mayer release. Directed by Victor Fleming. Screenplay by Sidney Howard, from the novel by Margaret Mitchell. Photographed by Ernest Haller. Principal cast members: Clark Gable, Vivien Leigh, Olivia de Havilland, Leslie Howard, Hattie McDaniel.

Clara Bow in *Hula* was made during Fleming's romance with the "It Girl" in 1927. Copyright 1927 by Paramount-Famous-Lasky Corporation.

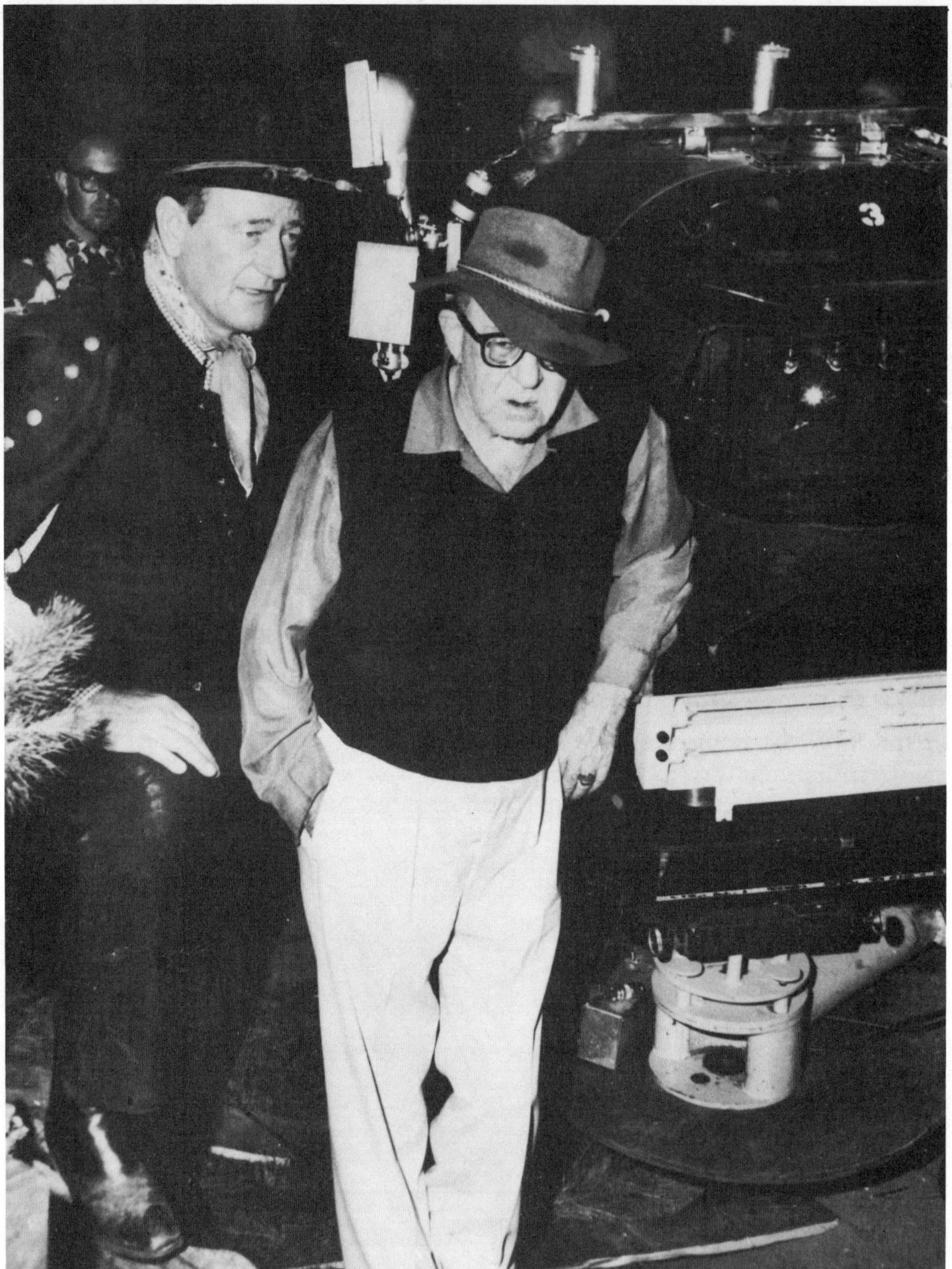

John Ford with John Wayne on the *How the West Was Won* set (1963). Copyright 1963 by Cinerama Corporation.

1940

John Ford
for The Grapes of Wrath

Mine eyes have seen the glory of the coming of the Lord;
He is trampling out the vintage where the grapes of wrath are stored . . .

From this Civil War song, *The Battle Hymn of the Republic,* John Steinbeck took the title for his 1939 best-selling novel. The following year, John Ford turned the story into one of his most celebrated motion pictures.

The picture itself lost out to Alfred Hitchcock's *Rebecca* in the academy voting, but the membership did give Oscars to Jane Darwell as the best supporting actress and to John Ford as the director of *The Grapes of Wrath.*

The film, a critical success in its day, has not stood up well with modern critics. British critic David Thompson calls it "an appalling posture of stoicism." Others have condemned it as overly sentimental, too romantic, and even as "a stupid capitalistic attempt to show liberalism."

Critics who are old enough to remember the period shown in *The Grapes of Wrath* do not share these views. Bosley Crowther, long-time *New York Times* critic, said that today's critics downgrade the film because it is not a harsh enough protest against social and economic inequalities.

The Grapes of Wrath is a story of social protest, but it shows such protest as it happened in 1933. The screaming, cursing mobs of the 1960s were a different breed entirely from the numbed, bitter people of the early depression years. To depict them otherwise is to distort history.

The family unit was still strong in the rural sections of America in the early 1930s. At that time and to those people, Ma Joad's struggle to keep her family together was not the "sickening sentiment" one modern critic called it. It was bitter realism. Those who grew up in the southwest in this period can recall numerous women like her.

These people were Okies—a term applied sneeringly to Oklahomans by Californians who did not want them in their Sunshine State. The Okies were farmers driven off their land by foreclosures and droughts. They migrated to California to seek work picking fruit. They clung together because they had only themselves for support.

The story was quite a contrast to Ford's previous work, including his Westerns and adventure films like *The Black Watch* (1929). The film opens with Tom Joad (Henry Fonda) returning home after four years in prison. He finds his family being driven off their farm and preparing to move in a rattletrap truck to California. Their trip along Highway 66 is as much an epic in its own way as the trek of *The Covered Wagon* to Oregon, shown in the famous 1923 film, and a much more bitter one.

Grandpa and grandma die on the way. A baby is born to Rose O'Sharon. There are no Indians to fight, but hostile California police want to prevent them from moving in. This was a time when local Chambers of Commerce posted signs to migrants, "Don't stop here. We can't take care of our own." Yet, when they stop in migrant camps, someone brings out a fiddle and there is dancing and a brave attempt to find some pleasure in a harsh life.

Henry Fonda was Tom Joad in Ford's *The Grapes of Wrath*, the film that earned Ford his second director's Oscar. Copyright 1940 by Twentieth Century-Fox Film Corporation.

***The Black Watch* (1929) had Victor McLaglen and Myrna Loy in a John Ford adventure film. Lumsden Hare assisted Ford as dialogue director on this early talkie. Copyright 1929 by Fox Film Corporation.**

The Joads move on through the migrant camps. Troubles come from the growing militancy of the emerging labor movement. Finally, Tom is involved in a strike when a man is killed. He slips in to tell his mother goodby before he flees because, as a convicted felon on parole, he knows he has no chance to clear himself.

As Ma Joad, Jane Darwell took the Academy Award for best supporting actress. Many who read the book thought Beulah Bondi would have been better, but Darwell made a heroic figure of the aging Oklahoma farmer's wife. Henry Fonda—surpassing his roles in *Mr. Roberts, Young Abe Lincoln,* or even the comedy classic, *My Lady Eve*—reached his peak as Tom Joad. Russell Simpson, John Carradine, Charley Grapewin, and the rest of the cast were equally good

The photography was semi-documentary; many saw it as a copy of *The Plow That Broke the Plains*, the government-sponsored Dust Bowl documentary of 1936. Ford received a lot of good comment on his use of background sounds—the hiss of steam from the truck's tortured radiator, the mournful whistle of a distant freight, the clatter of pans and dishes in the camps. Such noises were not as common as they later became after Ford introduced so much character-setting sound. In the early days of sound, noise, except for the rattle of machine guns and similar sound effects, was eliminated to prevent clash with the dialogue. Ford raised the use of noise to an art in this film.

Since making *The Informer* in 1935, Ford had directed Will Rogers in *Steamboat Round the Bend* (1935), *The Prisoner of Shark Island* (1936), *Mary of Scotland* (1936) with Katharine Hepburn, *The Plow and the Stars* (1937), and *Wee Willie Winkie* (1937) with Shirley Temple. In 1938 he made the hit *The Hurricane*, and then *Four Men and a Prayer* and *Submarine Patrol*. The next year brought the historic *Stagecoach*, the picture that made John Wayne a star, *Young Mr. Lincoln*, and *Drums Along the Mohawk*.

From Shirley Temple to Katharine Hepburn, from droll, folksy Will Rogers to somber Henry Fonda, and from *Wee Willie Winkie* to the epic sweep of *The Hurricane*,—it is hard to find a director who showed more versatility than John Ford did in the thirties and forties.

The Grapes of Wrath (1940), produced by Darryl F. Zanuck for Twentieth Century-Fox Film Corporation release. Directed by John Ford. Screenplay by Nunnally Johnson, from the book by John Steinbeck. Photographed by Gregg Toland. Principal cast members: Henry Fonda, Jane Darwell, Charley Grapewin, John Carradine.

John Ford's *Stagecoach* (1939) was the film that made a star of John Wayne, shown here with Claire Trevor. Copyright 1939 by United Artists Corporation.

John Ford and Peter Bogdanovich discuss Ford's films.

1941

John Ford
for How Green Was My Valley

At a meeting, John Ford once introduced himself with, "I'm John Ford. I make westerns."

Well, he did make westerns—an enormous number of them between 1917 and his final pictures in the 1960s. Many were quickies for Universal. Then, with Fox, he began to expand with films like *The Iron Horse* (1924), *Three Bad Men* (1926), and the semi-western *Cameo Kirby* (1923). In the middle of his career, Ford turned away from westerns, not returning to them until the last years of his long career as a director.

None of his four Academy Awards for direction was for a western. So, although much of modern film criticism centers on Ford as a maker of westerns, he was an all-around film maker, at home with every kind of film except pornography. His pictures were always characterized by a good sense of story value, well developed action, and revealing touches of character. He deserved to be the legend he was.

Ford was one of those rate film-makers who was commercial but still able to interest critics who often favor the less commercial productions. Of course, Ford had his box office troubles on occasion. *The Informer*, one of his best pictures, was saved from financial failure only because he made it so cheaply.

Ford is on record as saying he never had full control of his films, but his claim was not true. He was in control most of the time and did pretty much as he pleased. John Wayne said once that Ford could be "pretty mean at times." And then there is the often repeated story of Ford's answer to the supervisor who informed him that the director was three pages behind in his shooting. Ford ripped three pages from the script and said, "Now, we are on schedule. Beat it!"

Ford claimed that his best silent, *The Iron Horse* (1924), was ruined by a producer who insisted on inserting too many close-ups of Madge Bellamy. This is a figment of Ford's imagination. Any such excessive displays of the actress's pretty face must have been in the first previews, for they do not show in the prints in general release.

Throughout his career, Ford did pretty much as he pleased. When he couldn't get his way, he immediately got sick and did not come back, leaving the interfering producer or recalcitrant star to find another director. This happened on *Mister Roberts* following his arguments with Henry Fonda, and again on *Pinky* when Ford refused to continue working with Ethel Waters.

He was also known for "cutting in the camera," producing so little extra film that the editors had to use Ford's version of the picture.

In 1940, Ford had won the director's Oscar for *The Grapes of Wrath* but lost the best picture award to *Rebecca*. The following year, he again won the director's Oscar and also took the best picture award with *How Green Was My Valley*. The excellence of this picture can be seen from its competition: *Citizen Kane, Here Comes Mr. Jordan, The Little Foxes*, and *Sergeant York*.

How Green Was My Valley shows the decay of a community and the breaking up of the Morgan family. It is told as the reminiscenses of Huw Morgan, played as a boy by thirteen-year-old Roddy McDowell, with Rhys Williams as the adult Huw supplying the off-screen narration. Mr. Morgan (Donald Crisp in an Academy Award performance of his own) works with his three sons in the local coal mine. They all hope that Huw will go on to something better.

The sons turn to unionism, which the father abhors. This causes the sons to drift away to other places. Huw's sister (Maureen O'Hara) loves the minister (Walter Pidgeon). When marriage to him is impossible, she crosses the class barrier and marries the son of a mine operator. Huw has to go into the mines after his brothers leave, for his father's meager salary cannot support the family. The mine operators have consistently refused to keep up the property and Mr. Morgan is killed as a result of the antiquated machinery. During this time, the village has grown increasingly shabby. The adult Huw decides to leave the village, but, reflecting upon the character of his father, he observes, "Men like my father cannot die . . . They remain a living truth in my mind."

Olive Borden, George O'Brien, and J. Farrell MacDonald were in Ford's *Three Bad Men*. Copyright 1926 by Fox Film Corporation.

The venerable stage production *Cameo Kirby*, previously filmed with Dustin Farnum by Lasky Feature Play Company, was a vehicle for John Gilbert and Wallace Beery. Copyright 1923 by Fox Film Corporation.

Ford's mine set for *How Green Was My Valley* reproduced a section of Wales in California. Copyright 1941 by Twentieth Century-Fox Film Corporation.

The film is rich in incidents and character-revealing scenes that are a joy to watch. The mine owner coming to ask for the miner's daughter to marry his son, the wedding party, the sons dropping their meager pay into their mother's aproned lap, and the interplay between family members are all memorable John Ford touches. They show why he is a screen legend.

How Green Was My Valley (1941), produced by Darryl F. Zanuck for Twentieth Century-Fox Film Corporation release. Directed by John Ford. Screenplay by Philip Dunne, from the novel by Richard Llewellyn. Photographed by Arthur Miller. Principal cast members: Walter Pidgeon, Maureen O'Hara, Donald Crisp, Roddy McDowall, John Loder, Sara Allgood, Patric Knowles, Anna Lee.

After four close misses, William Wyler got his first Oscar for the wartime soap opera *Mrs. Miniver*. Copyright 1966 by Twentieth Century-Fox Film Corporation.

1942

William Wyler for Mrs. Miniver

Carl Laemmle, during the years he headed Universal, put so many relatives on the payroll that he was known throughout the industry as Uncle Carl. While Laemmle became rather eccentric as he aged, he was still canny enough to determine the jobs for his relatives and to see that they were not overpaid.

So it was that the best eighteen-year-old Will Wyler (b. 1902) could get was the position of flunky, carrying film cans in Universal's exchange office at 1600 Broadway, New York. Willy was paid twenty five dollars, from which Uncle Carl, ever the businessman, had five dollars a week extracted to pay for Willy's passage from Europe.

It all began for young Willy in 1920 when Uncle Carl took a trip back to his native Germany. Melanie Wyler, Willy's mother, immediately took a train from her native Alsace to see her cousin Carl. In the fashion of Jewish mothers who have problem sons, she poured out her troubles to Cousin Carl. She implored the rich American to save Willy from the temptations of Paris by taking him to America.

And so Willy Wyler went to New York to carry film for Cousin Carl. After a couple of years in New York, Willy somehow got himself transferred to Hollywood.

Lap-dissolve to 1941: Willy, told that his name sounded juvenile, has now become William Wyler. Behind him lie two decades of moviemaking in which he advanced from grinding out two-reel westerns to the highly regarded position of director.

Wyler's better pictures up to this time included *These Three*, the Lillian Hellman shocker, with Joel Macrea, Merle Oberon, Miriam Hopkins, and Bonita Granville; *Come and Get It*, the Edna Ferber story, with Edward Arnold and Walter Brennan; *Dead End*, which introduced the long-lived Dead End Kids; *Jezebel*, Bette Davis's Academy Award role; and *The Westerner*, in which Walter Brennan as Judge Roy Bean overshadowed the star, Gary Cooper.

In addition to these successful films, Wyler had also received four Academy Award nominations for directing *Dodsworth* (1936), with Walter Huston and Mary

Astor; *Wuthering Heights* (1939), which introduced Laurence Olivier to the American audience; and *The Little Foxes* (1941), with Bette Davis.

Unfortunately for Wyler, the Academy voters preferred Frank Capra for *Mr. Deeds Goes to Town* in 1936, Victor Fleming for *Gone With The Wind* in 1939, and John Ford for *How Green Was My Valley* in 1941. Then Wyler got a break that would end his losing streak and eventually move him into the select ranks of those who have won more than two Oscars for direction.

Sidney Franklin, a fine director from the silent days, had become an MGM producer after the death of Irving Thalberg in 1937. Human interest was his strong point. In addition to finishing *The Good Earth* after Thalberg died, Franklin was also responsible for *Random Harvest* and *Goodbye Mr. Chips*. Franklin had just been handed some *New Yorker* sketches about the trials of a British family during the early days of World War II. There was no story line in the sketches, but Franklin hired James Hilton (who wrote *Lost Horizon*), George Froeschel, Claudine West, and Arthur Wimperis to provide a story line. The result was *Mrs. Miniver*, the most popular film released in 1942.

The story itself was hardly a story. It chronicled the deprivations and dangers of a typical British family during the German blitz on London. At least, the promotion called the Minivers typical, but the only thing typical about them was Hollywood's usual tendency to exaggerate. Woven through the troubles of Mrs. Miniver was a subplot that was almost another story in itself. This was the romance of Richard Ney, playing the Minivers' oldest son, and Teresa Wright. As the story moves to a climax, we can sense a coming tragedy in Wyler's buildup implying that the son will be killed in the war. But there is a twist: it is the girl who is killed during an air raid.

The picture was released during the darkest days of the war. Great Britain was staggering, and the United States had just been blasted into the conflict by the Japanese devastation of Pearl Harbor. The picture, therefore, carried a

Dead End, with Humphrey Bogart and the Dead End Kids, was made by Wyler during his Goldwyn period. Copyright 1937 by Samuel Goldwyn Productions.

***Jezebel* failed to bring Wyler an Oscar, but it earned one for Bette Davis. Copyright 1938 by Vitagraph Incorporated.**

Walter Pidgeon and Greer Garson headed the cast in *Mrs. Miniver*, the public's favorite film for 1942. Copyright 1942 by Metro-Goldwyn-Mayer.

definite message: "It can happen *here*!" Those who flocked to see it hoped that, if the bombs did start falling on American cities as they had on London and Pearl Harbor, they could face their fear as bravely as Greer Garson and Walter Pidgeon had.

Mrs. Miniver was a product of its time, but looking at it now, the film was not that good. Art would have been better served if Wyler had received his first Oscar for *Jezebel* or *Dodsworth*. However, having won once, he would go on to greater glory.

Mrs. Miniver (1942), produced by Sidney Franklin for Metro-Goldwyn-Mayer release. Directed by William Wyler. Screenplay by Arthur Wimperis, George Froeschel, James Hilton, and Claudine West, from the book by Jan Strother. Photographed by Joseph Ruttenberg. Principal cast members: Walter Pidgeon, Greer Garson, Teresa Wright, Richard Ney, Dame May Whitty.

From the swagger of *Captain Blood* to the intrigue of *Casablanca* to the homey humor of *Life with Father*, Michael Curtiz seldom failed to give his audiences entertainment of a high order.

1943

Michael Curtiz for Casablanca

Michael Curtiz (1888–1962) was a Christmas present, born on 25 December 1888 in Budapest, Hungary. He supposedly became stagestruck after carrying a spear in an opera performance when he was eleven years old.

He later became an actor, and, at one time, took a turn as a circus clown when roles were hard to come by. World War I got him into the Hungarian army, where he was wounded fighting on the Russian front. It was a fortunate wound. It rendered him unfit for front-line duty and he was placed, because of his stage background, in charge of an official newsreel company.

Excited by the possibilities of films, he went to Paris after the war and became a director. An example of his work during this time is *Sodom and Gomorrah*, a spectacle using the DeMille flashback technique. In it, a wicked woman of today (Lucy Doraine) has a vision of her past life in Sodom and is reformed.

In 1926, Curtiz met Harry Warner of the Warner Brothers studio in Paris. Warner was impressed and brought Curtiz to Hollywood. He established himself quickly and remained with Warner Brothers for twenty-six years. According to the Curtiz legend, Michael hung out around night courts to learn about America, claiming, "In these places you see the real emotions of people."

After sound came in, Curtiz directed the part-talking *Noah's Ark* (1928), a flop with George O'Brien and Dolores Costello. This was followed by seven years of profitable, but hardly artistic, triumphs.

Then, in 1935, he made *Captain Blood*, which introduced Errol Flynn in his first major role on the American screen. The films that followed made Curtiz and Flynn the joint kings of the swashbucklers. Their enormous popularity showed that a successful film does not depend upon star and director liking each other. But, although Curtiz made his American reputation with movies like *Robin Hood* (1938), he also sandwiched in such fine musicals as *Yankee Doodle Dandy* (1942), in which James Cagney superbly impersonated George M. Cohan; *Mildred Pierce* (1946), which brought Joan Crawford her Oscar; and *Life With Father* (1947), with William Powell.

Motion picture historians will probably remember Curtiz best not for the long line of stars he directed, stretching from Dolores Costello and Bette Davis to Elvis Presley but, for *Casablanca*, the wartime espionage film he made in 1943.

The test of a director is not what he does, but what he does with his material—story, cast, and photographer.

Curtiz certainly had the best of all three in this picture, and he did his best with them, turning out one of the classic films of the 1940s. The direction was so skillful that the individual parts of the picture fitted together seamlessly. The cast did not seem to be a cast. They became living people—and, in 1943, our sympathies were entirely with them. Judging by the number of times *Casablanca* has reappeared on TV, modern audiences must like it as well as we did then. No small item in the film's success was the recurrence of the song "As Time Goes By." This reprise was not stuck in casually. It was a reminder to the star of the woman he had lost and who had now come to him for help.

Casablanca is the story of the owner of Rick's American Bar in Casablanca (Humphrey Bogart), an ex-soldier of fortune. A bitter man, he claims he no longer cares for anyone but himself. Then into his life comes Lisa, the woman he had once loved and lost (Ingrid Bergman). Her husband, Victor Laszlo, (Paul Henreid) is an underground leader who must get to Portugal to escape pursuing Nazis. The Laszlos need letters of transit to get out of Casablanca and onto a plane for Lisbon. Rick has two such letters given to him by Ugarte (Peter Lorre), who is then shot.

Rick wants nothing to do with the Laszlos, but each time his pianist, Sam (Dooley Wilson), plays "As Time Goes By," the memory of the old romance in Paris haunts him. Because Lisa deserted him, he refuses to give her the letters of transit. Then, in a confrontation between them, she tells Rick that she was already married to Laszlo when she fell in love with Rick. She thought Laszlo

Superb art direction, like this sea battle scene, added greatly to the appeal of *Captain Blood*, the film that made Errol Flynn a star. Copyright 1935 by Warner Brothers Pictures Corporation.

Dolores Costello (Mrs. John Barrymore) and Ralph Graves were in Curtiz's *Glad Rag Doll*. Copyright 1929 by Warner Brothers Pictures Corporation.

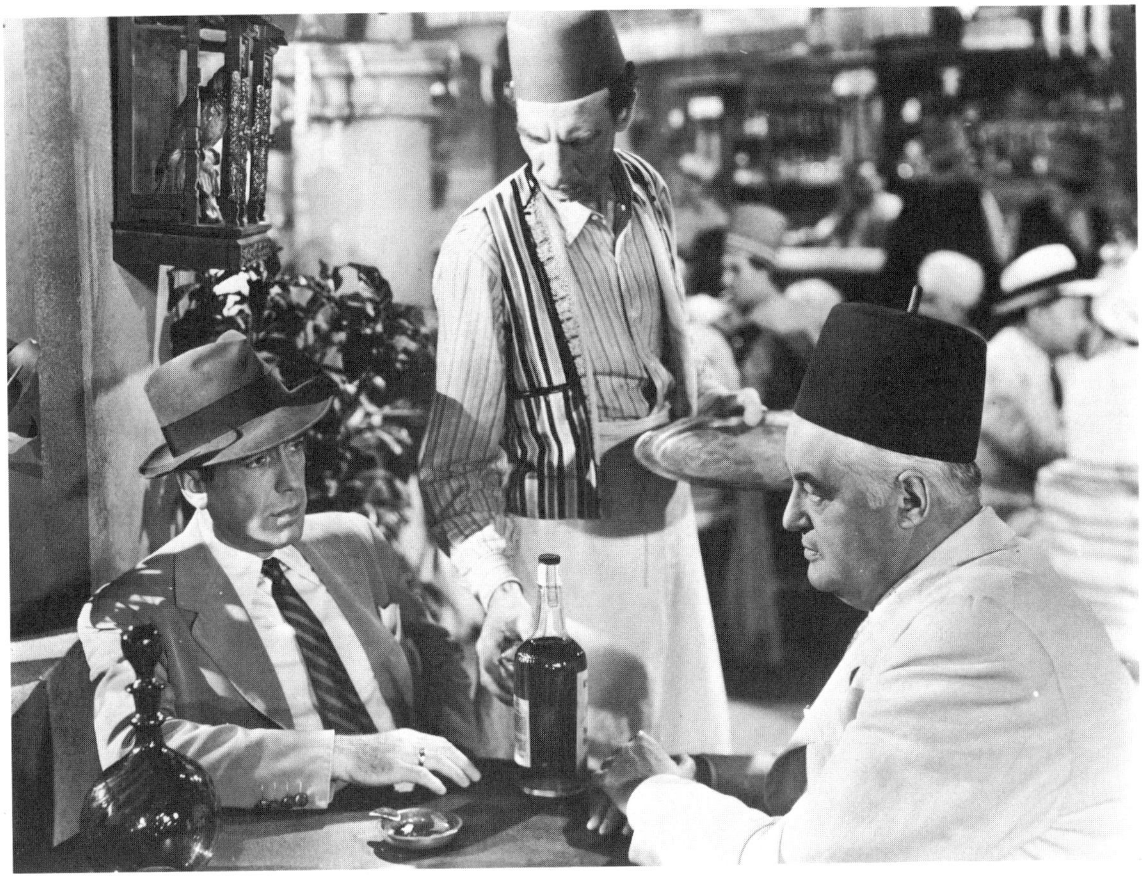

Humphrey Bogart, Oliver Pritchett, and Sydney Greenstreet in the classic *Casablanca*. Copyright 1942 by Warner Brothers Pictures Corporation.

dead, but, when he returned, Lisa felt honor-bound to return to him although she actually loved Rick.

Convinced by the story, Rick sets out to help her and Laszlo get away, opposed by Nazi Major Strasser (Conrad Veidt). Weaving through the ensuing intrigue are Sydney Greenstreet as a black marketeer, and Claude Rains, in a superior performance, as the local prefect of police. In the end, after killing Strasser, putting the woman he loved and her husband on the plane for Lisbon, Bogart walk off with Rains into the misty night.

The stock phrase, "Play it again, Sam," became as much a Bogart trademark as "Take me to ze Casbah" was for Charles Boyer—phrases neither of them actually said. Our regret is that Bergman, Bogart, Rains, Greenstreet, Henreid, and Curtiz never played it again as they did in this fine picture.

Casablanca (1943), produced by Hal Wallis for release by Warner Brothers Picture Corporation. Directed by Michael Curtiz. Screenplay by Julius Epstein, Philip Epstein, and Howard Koch. Photographed by Arthur Edeson. Principal cast members: Humphrey Bogart, Ingrid Bergman, Paul Henreid, Claude Rains, Conrad Veidt, Sydney Greenstreet, Dooley Wilson as "Sam," who played it again.

Leo McCarey directs Victor Moore in *Make Way for Tomorrow,* one of McCarey's less successful efforts. Copyright 1937 by Paramount Pictures Incorporated.

1944

Leo McCarey for Going My Way

Leo McCarey told a lot of stories about his career, such as starting as a script girl and being chased out of the law profession by an irate client, plus many others. In evaluating these, we must remember that McCarey was a gag writer, comedy director, and an associate of Hal Roach and Laurel and Hardy.

None of these is any guarantee of truthfulness. However, a gentleman who knew McCarey quite well has assured us that Leo had more integrity than most Hollywood figures who talk about their past. Leo always insisted upon having at least 3 percent truth in every story he told.

However, there does seem to be some truth in his claim that *Going My Way* was inspired by an actual person. McCarey claimed that he was approached by an old priest who wanted donations for his church. Leo asked him how long he had been with the church.

"Forty-five years!" the old man said proudly. "I built that church myself."

McCarey asked how the old man got along with the young priests.

"They are all right," he said. "but I think they are already figuring on how to change things when I die."

This amused McCarey. "I didn't know it then," he said later, "but right then I was meeting the Barry Fitzgerald character in *Going My Way*."

The idea germinated, and, eventually, McCarey wrote a script which he called *The Padre*. It was about an old priest who presides over a church that is heavily in debt. The bishop, not wanting to hurt the old man's feelings, sends in a young priest to solve the financial trouble. McCarey approached Bing Crosby to play the role of the young priest.

Crosby insisted that the public would never accept him in such a part. McCarey argued that Bing said the same thing when Jack Knapp of Decca wanted the singer to record "*Adeste Fidelis*" and "*Silent Night*". That record turned out to be one of Crosby's greatest hits.

Crosby finally agreed. This off-beat casting was followed by another choice just as startling. For the aged priest, McCarey chose Barry Fitzgerald, late of the Abbey Players in Dublin. Fitzgerald had never played anything on the American screen except boozy old men. He was as unlikely a priest as Crosby.

McCarey once said that he was able to get the picture financed by Paramount because Buddy G. DeSylva, an ex-song writer then the production head, knew absolutely nothing about priests and did not realize how ridiculous casting Crosby and Fitzgerald was for such a film.

But, when the Academy Awards were handed out, *Going My Way* took the awards for top picture, top star, top supporting actor, and top director. About McCarey's Oscar, one voter said, "I voted for him. Anybody who can get two boozers like Crosby and Fitzgerald to act like convincing priests deserves all honors you can give him."

The script, as written by Frank Butler and Frank Cavett from McCarey's story, tells how Father O'Malley (Crosby) is sent to do something about Father Fitzgibbon's (Fitzgerald) rundown parish. Like the old priest McCarey had met, Fitzgibbon had led his flock for forty-five years. There is some friction between the two, but O'Malley enlists the aid of a boys' choir and an opera singer (Rise Stevens) to help him sell a song to pay the church debts. We are given the impression that O'Malley and the opera star were rather close before he decided to become a priest.

Then the church burns down, and more money is needed. O'Malley gets help from a local builder (Gene Lockhart) and inspires the community to rebuild the church. O'Malley is then ready to move on to another place where his troubleshooting abilities are needed. As his last gesture, he brings over from Ireland Fitzgibbon's old mother, whom he has been longing to see.

Frank McHugh, Bing Crosby, and Rise Stevens in *Going My Way,* which brought Leo McCarey his second director's Oscar. Copyright 1944 by Paramount Pictures Corporation.

Bing Crosby repeated his priest's role with Ingrid Bergman in *The Bells of St. Mary's.* Copyright 1945 by RKO-Radio Pictures, Incorporated.

Good Sam, with Joan Loring and Gary Cooper, was one of McCarey's less successful pictures. Copyright 1948 by RKO-Radio Pictures, Incorporated.

Going My Way is saturated with sentiment, but it is a delightful sentiment that combines just the right amount of comedy and pathos. The picture was both a critical and a popular success. Now a staple on late-night TV, the film is still enjoyable to watch, for its thirty-five years rest lightly upon it.

After *Going My Way*, McCarey hit again with *The Bells of St. Mary's* in 1945. Crosby continued his O'Malley role opposite Ingrid Bergman as a nun. According to one report, *Bells* on its first showing played to 41,000,000 paid admissions while *Gone With the Wind* played to only 37,500,000.

McCarey was to make only five more pictures, before his death in 1969. Without question, he made the world a brighter place through his pictures.

Going My Way (1944), produced by Leo McCarey for Paramount Picture Corporation release. Directed by Leo McCarey. Screenplay by Frank Butler and Frank Cavett, from an original story by Leo McCarey. Principal cast members: Bing Crosby, Barry Fitzgerald, Rise Stevens, Frank McHugh, Gene Lockhart.

Taking the cameraman's seat, Billy Wilder symbolizes that he is always the man in the saddle in his films.

1945

Billy Wilder for The Lost Weekend

Billy Wilder is not Willy Wyler, although he is often mistaken for his fellow director. In fact, Billy isn't Billy, either. He's Sam. Sam Wilder was born in Vienna in 1906, and his fond family envisioned him as a lawyer. One year in the University of Vienna was enough to convince Sam that he could find a better way to spend his future.

He went to Berlin to work on a newspaper and began writing movie scripts that no one would buy. There is a somewhat improbable tale about how he finally sold his first one. In assessing this story, remember that Mr. Wilder is a writer, a producer, and a director. Any one of the three is suspect when telling about his past, but when all three are combined in the same man, believe what he says at your own risk. As this story goes, a movie producer was surprised by a returning husband and ran into Wilder's apartment to hide. The enterprising writer used the opportunity to sell him a script.

After this coup, Wilder remained in the German film industry until the rise of Hitler sent him fleeing to Paris. He was not a success with the French, and, by 1933, was in Hollywood trying to write scripts in German for translation into English. He worked on five films before Ernst Lubitsch teamed Wilder with fellow writer Charles Brackett for *Bluebeard's Eighth Wife* (1938) with Claudette Colbert and Gary Cooper. This was the beginning of a long and fruitful association. It included *Sunset Boulevard* and *Ninotchka*, among others.

Wilder, who always resented what others did to his scripts, became a director in 1942 with *The Major and the Minor*, which he and Brackett also wrote, an amusing film with Ray Milland and Ginger Rogers. It was followed by *Five Graves to Cairo*, with Eric Von Stroheim impersonating the German general Rommel; *Double Indemnity* (1944), the splendidly done filming of James M. Cain's hard-boiled book; and, in 1945, *The Lost Weekend*. Wilder broke his partnership with Brackett to work with Raymond Chandler on *Double Indemnity*, but was back with Brackett on *The Lost Weekend*, which would earn best film, best actor, and best director awards.

The Lost Weekend, based on Charles R. Jackson's novel, is a harrowing tale of an alcoholic's misery. It turned out to be actor Ray Milland's picture; the rest of the cast has been forgotten. Milland's was a one-man performance, with the other actors merely feeding him cues for his lines. It was definitely a message picture, but somehow audiences of 1945, while gripped by its story, viewed the alcoholic with detachment. "I think I'll go throw a 'lost weekend,'" they joked when contemplating a drunken vacation.

In *Lost Weekend*, Don Birnam (Milland) is a failed writer who has turned to the bottle. The picture, following the novel except for a more upbeat ending, traces Birnam's final degradation as his girl, Helen (Jane Wyman), and friends try to get him off the bottle. We see the ingenious places he hides his liquor, and then, when his money runs out, how he tries to steal a woman's handbag in a bar. Then we follow him down mean streets as he tries to hock his typewriter, but is frustrated because it is a Jewish holiday and the pawnshops are closed. Later, he falls down the stairs and ends up in the alcoholic ward of a hospital where the horrors of delirium tremens are graphically depicted. Getting out of the hospital, he steals Helen's coat to hock so he can get his gun out of pawn and kill himself. Then, in the only major departure from the book, she talks him out of this, and he starts the long climb back up again.

The picture was both a critical and a financial success. With *Double Indemnity* and *The Lost Weekend* back-to-back, Wilder was hailed as a directorial genius. He was then given *The Emperor Waltz* (1948), which proved to be one of

Ginger Rogers (right) masquerades as a young girl with Diana Lynn in *The Major and the Minor*, the first film Billy Wilder directed in the United States. Copyright 1942 by Paramount Pictures Incorporated.

Ray Milland gave the performance of his life as the alcoholic in *The Lost Weekend*. Copyright 1945 by Paramount Pictures Corporation.

One of Wilder's less successful films matched aging Gary Cooper with girlish Audrey Hepburn in *Love in the Afternoon.* Copyright 1957 by Allied Artists.

Bing Crosby's worst films. However, one flop never destroys a genius. Wilder was set for still greater triumphs, as well as more flops like *Love in the Afternoon* (1945).

The Lost Weekend (1945), produced by Charles Brackett for Paramount Pictures Corporation release. Directed by Billy Wilder. Screenplay by Billy Wilder and Charles Brackett, from the novel by Charles F. Jackson. Photographed by John F. Seitz. Principal cast members: Ray Milland, Jane Wyman, Philip Terry, Howard DaSilva.

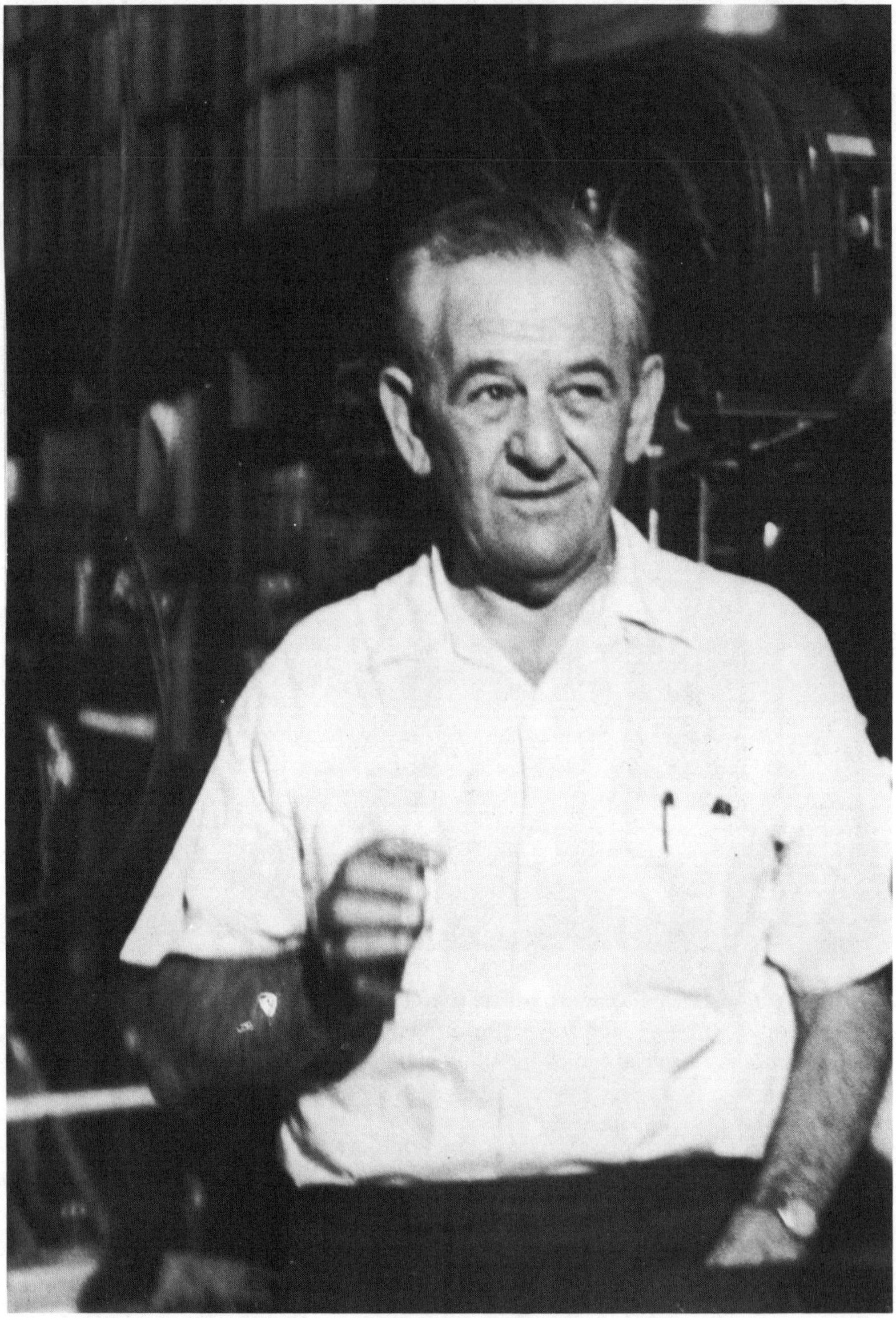

William Wyler won the second of his three Oscars for *The Best Years of Our Lives.*

1946

William Wyler
for The Best Years of Our Lives

Like *Mrs. Miniver, The Best Years of Our Lives,* William Wyler's second Oscar winner, was the product of its time. The United States went into World War II not yet fully recovered from the traumatic shock of the great depression of the 1930s. The war drew ten million men into the armed services. At the war's end, the bulk of them returned to civilian life again and created many problems. It is a sad, cruel fact of life that the returning soldier is surplus goods. Nobody really wants him; those who stayed behind have the permanent jobs; industry is cutting back from the pressure of war production. In addition to these economic problems, there are the natural tensions and anxieties that a return to civil life brings to a mass of men after mustering out.

The boys who went to war returned as men. The soda jerk who left came back a man, ready to find his proper place in society—a society that often did not know what to do with him. Many of those who returned did not find a place for themselves. Others found their places with difficulty. In many cases, the adjustment was difficult.

The Best Years of Our Lives sketched this problem of all returning soldiers by focusing upon the lives of three such men. The idea of the film originated with Samuel Goldwyn after he saw a picture of returning Marines in *Life* Magazine. He wondered what the effect would be upon the men and their families. He commissioned McKinley Kantor to write a story which William Wyler, a favorite director of Goldwyn's turned into the academy's choice for best picture and best director.

The three returning service men are Dana Andrews who discovers that the war bride he married is a tart; Fredric March who is a junior banker in conflict with his boss over liberal GI loans; and Harold Russell, a double amputee who fears that his fiancée regards him with pity rather than love. March won the best actor award for his role.

Harold Russell, a real-life double amputee, received a supporting actor Academy Award, but it was Dana Andrew who had the most moving role in the picture. While the entire picture was a tableau of excellent scenes, two of

Andrews's are as good as the best ever filmed. One shows the unhappy man, broken-up over his failures, going to a wrecked bomber in the junk pile at the local airport. He climbs into the cockpit, and, for a few brief moments, relives his time of glory and importance as a combat pilot. Wyler's superb use of the camera boom here actually suggests flying.

The other scene shows Andrews and March together. Andrews has taken up with March's daughter (Teresa Wright). March opposes this, and, when the two men talk in a bar, persuades Andrews to call the girl and break off their relationship. As the scene is played, March is at the piano watching Hoagy Carmichel teach Russell to play a tune with the hooks that are the prostheses for his hands. March keeps his eyes on this by-play while we see Andrews, in the background, go to the phone. We do not see his face nor hear what he says. We see him only in a long shot, with Carmichael and Russell, and March ignoring Andrews and watching them, in the foreground. Andrews completes his call and goes out without looking toward the others.

In this remarkable scene, Wyler "photographed thought," depicting and symbolizing the heartbreak of Andrews and the hope of Russell as he finds that he can do things he never thought he could do again. In the actions of Fredric March, we see the hurt of one returned veteran who is forced to act against another for what he believes is his daughter's best interest.

Wyler had packed a lot into scenes before, such as the interchange between Bette Davis and Herbert Marshall in *The Little Foxes* (1941), but never before or after did he put so much into a single scene as he did in this one. The effectiveness came not so much from the content of the scene as staged, but from what Wyler left to the audience's imagination by discarding the temptation to show closeups of Andrews' anguish.

Wyler, in shirt-sleeves under the boom, directs Walter Pidgeon and Greer Garson in a scene from *Mrs. Miniver*. Copyright 1942 by Metro-Goldwyn-Mayer.

Charles Dingle, Bette Davis, Carl Benton Reid, Patricia Collinge, and Herbert Marshall in *The Little Foxes*, a brutal portrait of a vicious woman. Copyright 1941 by Samuel Goldwyn Productions.

John Derr, Hoagy Carmichael, Harold Russell, and Dana Andrews in *The Best Years of Our Lives*. Copyright 1946 by Samuel Goldwyn Productions.

The Best Years of Our Lives (1946), produced by Samuel Goldwyn for United Artists Corporation release. Directed by William Wyler. Screenplay by Robert E. Sherwood from the story by McKinley Kantor. Photographed by Greg Toland. Principal cast members: Fredric March, Dana Andrews, Myrna Loy, Teresa Wright, Harold Russell, Virginia Mayo.

Elia Kazan won the 1947 director's Oscar for
Gentleman's Agreement.

1947

Elia Kazan for Gentleman's Agreement

Elia Kazan (b. 1909) comes by his sympathy for the oppressed more honestly than many of the liberals who have tried to use motion pictures to express their views. As an Anatolian Greek born in Turkey, Kazan was a genuine oppressed person, for his people were victims of hatred that often led to riots and massacres.

His father, a dealer in rugs, lived in Istanbul, the Turkish capital. Later, the family immigrated to the United States, where Elia Kazanjoglu grew up in a lower-middle-class section of New York's West Side. He was an outsider who did not get along well with others.

Later, he worked his way through Williams College as a waiter and dishwasher. This engendered hostility in him toward the wealthier and more gregarious students he served. This was one major reason why he joined the Communist Party while in college.

During his college years, Kazan saw the famous Russian movie *Potemkin*, and, for the first time, began to see motion pictures as something he might like to participate in. This led him to join a theater group and then to work with Lee Strasberg. Here, he worked with men like Clifford Odets and learned to analyze character and emotions. He directed his first play in 1934 and broke with the Communist Party in 1937. His first Broadway success as a director was Thornton Wilder's *The Skin of Our Teeth* in 1942. He followed with *One Touch of Venus* (1943) and *Jakobowsky and the Colonel* (1944). This brought him a bid to direct *A Tree Grows in Brooklyn* (1945), the Betty Smith best seller, for Fox. *A Tree Grows in Brooklyn* earned James Dunn a best supporting actor award.

The unsuccessful *Sea of Grass* (1947) and the successful *Boomerang* (1947) followed. Then Darryl F. Zanuck picked Kazan to direct *Gentleman's Agreement*. The film was based upon Laura Z. Hobson's best-selling novel and was the screen's first serious attempt to deal with the problem of anti-Semitism in the United States. Today, the picture is often criticized as being too mild and for failing to come to grips with its theme. Such criticism is unwarranted, for, here again, we must consider the picture in the context of its time. As such, it was decidedly a courageous picture, and a well-made one.

In this period of his career, Kazan had not obtained the artistic control of his films that he later enjoyed. Darryl F. Zanuck was the producer, and he was a strong personality who impressed his viewpoint on every frame of the picture. The picture was Zanuck's idea, and he made it against opposition of his own people. He selected Moss Hart to do the screen play, when Kazan preferred Lillian Hellman, who would have produced a tougher story.

The story line involves Phil Green (Gregory Peck), a journalist, who has been assigned to write a story on anti-Semitism in America. After some thought, he decides to pose as a Jew and to write his personal experiences under the title, "I Was a Jew for 6 Weeks."

In the course of his investigations, he encounters snubs and ostracism that he never realized existed. A series of incidents climax when he is refused entrance to a resort hotel. His situation is complicated as he gradually comes to realize that he has been an unconscious anti-Semite himself. His sweetheart, Kathy (Dorothy McGuire), the daughter of his publisher, is also an unconscious anti-Semite.

Unconscious means that the feeling was there, but the person has never admitted it nor does anything about it. This is brought out in a very effective scene in which Kathy tells a friend, Dave Goldman (John Garfield), about an anti-Semitic party she attended. He asks what she did. She replies that she was horrified. Dave shoots back, "But what did you *do*!"

As a make-believe Jew, Peck suffers inconvenience, mental persecutions, and social rejection. These appear searing enough; however, when measured against the horrors of the holocaust in Germany, they seem mild indeed. Since *Gentleman's Agreement* came at a time when the German horrors were still fresh in the public's mind, it did not appear that Peck suffered very much. This greatly weakened the effectiveness of the picture.

It was, however, tremendously applauded by the critics and was a box-office success as well.

Doc (Harry Carey) and the nurse (Nora Cecil) know something that Brewton (Spencer Tracy) doesn't know: The baby about to be born to his wife is not his. *The Sea of Grass* was Elia Kazan's second directorial effort. Copyright 1947 by Metro-Goldwyn-Mayer.

Boomerang (1947) was Elia Kazan's third film. This scene shows the murder of the priest (Wyrley Birch). Copyright 1947 by Twentieth Century-Fox Film Corporation.

Gregory Peck was the investigative reporter and Anne Revere was his mother in *Gentleman's Agreement*, Elia Kazan's Oscar-winning film. Copyright 1947 by Twentieth Century-Fox Film Corporation.

Gentleman's Agreement (1947), produced by Darryl F. Zanuck for Twentieth Century-Fox Film Corporation release. Directed by Elia Kazan. Screenplay by Moss Hart, from the novel by Laura Z. Hobson. Photographed by Arthur Miller. Principal cast members: Gregory Peck, Dorothy McGuire, Anne Revere, Celeste Holm, John Garfield.

John Huston as he appeared in 1953 while directing *Moulin Rouge*. Copyright 1953 by United Artists Corporation.

1948

John Huston
for The Treasure of the Sierra Madre

Quite often, movies and TV shows depict motion picture directors as rather strange and outlandish creatures. Before we dismiss this as exaggerated burlesque, it is well to consider Mr. John Huston.

Humphrey Bogart, who certainly should have been able to recognize an odd character since he was one himself, said that Huston had more color than most actors in Hollywood. Others, noting Huston's flamboyant taste in clothes, his peculiar manners, eccentricities, and often perverse sense of humor, have used stronger language in describing Huston. None deny, however, that, in his prime, he was a superb director.

Huston (b. 1906) was the child of the distinguished actor Walter Huston and a Memphis, Tennessee, newspaper woman. He apparently inherited abilities from both, for he was an exceptional screenwriter before he became a director. He had opportunities to pick up the rudiments of both writing and direction, for, after his parents divorced, he was shunted back and forth between them.

He did some acting in child's parts, but had a sickly childhood. He toughened up in his teens and became a lightweight prize fighter. Then he drifted back into acting for a while before going off for Mexico to join the Mexican cavalry. He seemed to have done more drinking than fighting during this escapade.

In 1929, twenty-three years old, he was back in New York. He wrote a play and some short stories. Then his mother got him a newspaper job from which he was fired for incompetency.

He next joined his father in Hollywood, but the job Walter got his son with Samuel Goldwyn did not pan out. He went to Universal and then to Warners, developing into one of the better screenwriters. He had a hand in the script for *The Amazing Dr. Clitterhouse*, with Bogart and Edward G. Robinson, and *Jezebel*, the Bette Davis Oscar film, and helped on *Sergeant York*.

Warners wanted him to work on *High Sierra*, the film that was to make Bogart a top star. Huston held out for the director's job and was promised a chance if he would work on *High Sierra*.

The picture was a hit, and he was handed Dashiell Hammett's mystery story *The Maltese Falcon* (1941). Huston wrote his own script and did some inspired casting with Bogart as Sam Spade, the private eye, Sydney Greenstreet as The Fat Man, and Mary Astor as the murderess. The story itself, based on a hunt for a valuable statuette, the Maltese falcon, was hardly realism, but Huston's taut, hard direction gave it a "you are there" quality that scored with audiences.

He then did *In This Our Life* (1942), with Bette Davis and Olivia de Havilland, and *Across the Pacific* (1942), with Bogart and Mary Astor, before going off to war to make documentary films. His first picture after his return was *Three Strangers* (1946). The next was *The Treasure of the Sierra Madre* (1948).

This was the picture that earned Huston his director's Oscar, and most will agree that he richly deserved it. It was a popular as well as a critical success, which was odd, considering that it was a definitely downbeat story, ending with the star's death.

The Maltese Falcon was Huston's first film as a director. It had a superb cast in Humphrey Bogart, Peter Lorre, Mary Astor, and Sydney Greenstreet. Copyright 1941 by Warner Brothers Pictures Corporation.

Humphrey Bogart had one of his greatest roles in *The Treasure of the Sierra Madre*. Copyright 1946 by Warner Brothers Pictures Corporation.

In *The Treasure of the Sierra Madre*, Howard (Walter Huston), a grizzled old prospector, sits around the flophouses in Tampico, Mexico, talking of gold in the mountains. this interests Fred Dobbs (Humphrey Bogart), an American bum. He and Bob Curtin (Tim Holt) manage a grubstake, and, with Howard, set out in search of gold.

When they find it, Dobbs's character begins to change. Formerly, he had been a likeable bum. Now the corrupting influence of gold brings out a character-destroying greed. Although they are threatened by a would-be claim jumper (Bruce Bennett), Indians, and Mexican bandits, it is clear that their greatest danger is Dobbs's treacherous nature.

Howard wanders off to aid some Indians with a sick child. Dobbs and Curtin start for the coast with their bag of gold dust. Dobbs tries to murder Curtin. He fails and goes on alone with the gold. Then, at the climax, he stretches out beside a waterhole to drink. A noise attracts his attention. He looks up to find he is surrounded by the Mexican bandits. He dies hard, and, during the final struggle and torture, the gold sack is upset, and wind blows the dust away.

The popular appeal of the film was in the taut direction that created a mounting suspense, the natural settings that provided total authenticity, and the believable characterizations by a superb cast. Intellectuals and reviewers who must have social significance before they will condescend to approve a picture delighted in Huston's contempt for materialism.

Although Huston made some highly successful pictures later, none surpassed *The Treasure of the Sierra Madre*. Huston made the total flop, *The Red Badge of Courage*, but he also gave us *The Asphalt Jungle*, which introduced Marilyn Monroe, *The African Queen*, with its superb pairing of Bogart and Katharine Hepburn, *Moulin Rouge* with Jose Ferrer as Toulouse Latrec, *Moby Dick* with Gregory Peck as Ahab, *The Misfits* with the unlikely pairing of Clark Gable and Marilyn Monroe, and the popular but poorly done *Night of the Iguana*. As for *The Bible*, in which he played Noah as well as directed, the best that can be said for it is that King James did it better.

The Treasure of the Sierra Madre (1948), produced by Henry Blanke, for Warners-First National release. Directed by John Huston. From the novel by B. Traven. Photographed by Ted McCord. Principal cast members: Humphrey Bogart, Walter Huston, Tim Holt, Bruce Bennett, Alfonso Bedoya.

John Huston as Noah leads the animals into the ark in *The Bible . . . in the Beginning*. Copyright 1966 by Twentieth Century-Fox Film Corporation.

Joseph L. Mankiewicz received his first Academy award nomination in 1932, but it took him seventeen years to finally get two. He received both the screenplay and director's awards for *A Letter to Three Wives.* Copyright 1949 by Twentieth Century-Fox Film Corporation.

1949

Joseph L. Mankiewicz for A Letter To Three Wives

An official biography of Joseph L. Mankiewicz (b. 1909) in the Margaret Herrick Library of the Academy of Motion Picture Arts and Sciences leaves the impression that Joe was called to Hollywood because of his outstanding work as a newspaperman.

Since this is "official," it must be correct. That means the story that Joseph L. got a job because his brother Herman promised to sober up and finish a screen play if his brother was hired is just another of those Hollywood legends. However, considering who Herman Mankiewicz was, the story is quite plausible. In fact, it is more probable than the official story.

In any event, Hollywood got a bargain in the Mankiewicz brothers. Both were brilliant screenwriters. Herman has credits ranging from collaborations with Tod Browning on Lon Chaney silents to the great *Citizen Kane,* which he wrote for Orson Welles.

Joe early showed his promise by copping an Oscar nomination for his *Skippy* screenplay in 1932. He lost out in the voting, but made up for it when he got both the screenplay and director's Oscars for *A Letter to Three Wives* in 1949, and then did an exact repeat the next year for *All about Eve.* That is a record no one has matched yet.

Joseph L. Mankiewicz was born in Wilkes-Barre, Pennsylvania. Then the family moved to New York where his father was a professor at City College of New York. A junior prodigy, Joseph graduated from high school at fifteen and from Columbia University at nineteen. He then went to Berlin to visit relatives and stayed to become European correspondent for the Chicago Tribune. He switched from this to translating titles for the movies which UFA, the German film company, imported to the United States.

In the meantime, brother Herman, who had been a drama critic for the New York *Times,* got a solid foothold in Hollywood as a writer. Brother Joe joined him in 1929 as an apprentice writer at sixty dollars a week. Sound was coming in. Joe wrote *Fast Company* and *Skippy* and developed quite a reputation as a screenwriter.

He wanted to direct, but Louis B. Mayer talked him out it. Mayer's advice was to keep writing and turn to producing, which he did at MGM and Fox. Fox finally gave him a chance to direct *Dragonwyck* (1946), with Gene Tierney and Vincent Price. He followed this with such films as *The Late George Apley* (1947), with Ronald Colman. After three other less notable films, he wrote and directed *A Letter to Three Wives*, the 1949 double-Oscar winner.

Looking back today at Oscar winners of a bygone era, it is not always clear what the academy voters had in mind. *A Letter to Three Wives* was a very good writing job, and that may have been what carried Mankiewicz to his director's Oscar as well. Mankiewicz can hardly claim total credit for the story. It was from a novel by John Klempner and was adapted for the screen by Vera Caspary, a noted novelist herself. However, it was Mankiewicz's genius for apt dialogue that carried the film. The wit sparkled. So, although the year's top picture award went to *All the King's Men*, Mankiewicz certainly deserved his screenplay Oscar, but why the academy membership thought the direction was better than William Wyler's work on *The Heiress*, with Olivia de Havilland giving a best actress Oscar winning performance, is something only the voters know.

The story of *A Letter to Three Wives* begins when Addie Ross, who is never seen (the voice is that of Celeste Holm), sends a letter to each of three wives in whose husbands she is interested. She says in each letter that, by the end of the day, she will elope with one of the husbands. The husband is not named. The

Vanessa Brown tips Ronald Colman a wink as she brings Richard Haydn to the altar in *The Late George Apley*, Joseph L. Mankiewicz's second picture as a director. Copyright 1947 by Twentieth Century-Fox Film Corporation.

The mailman delivers the fateful letter to Linda Darnell, Ann Sothern, and Jeanne Crain in Mankiewicz's *A Letter to Three Wives.* Copyright 1949 by Twentieth Century-Fox Film Corporation.

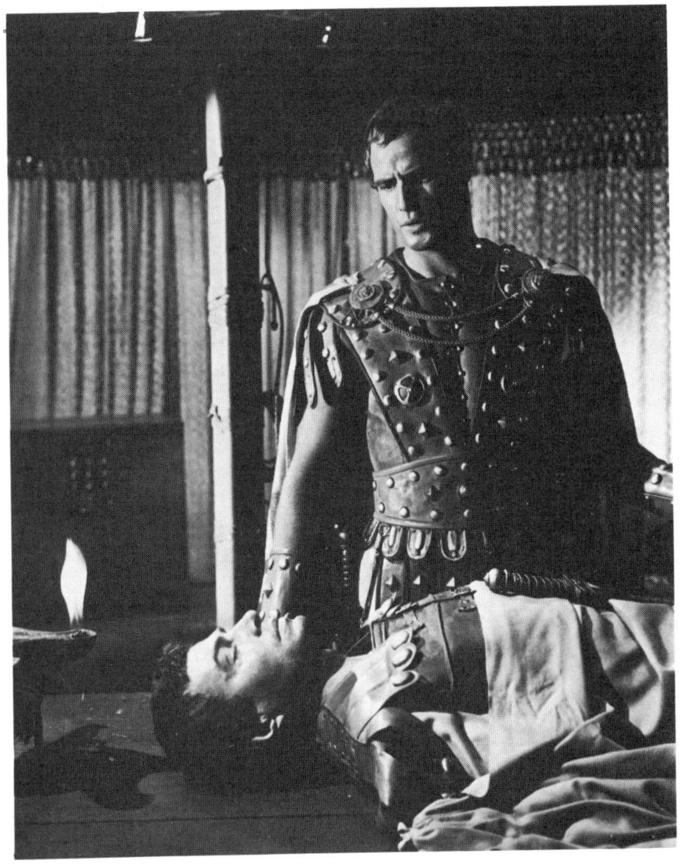

Mankiewicz did a creditable job with Shakespeare's *Julius Caesar,* with Marlon Brando as Anthony and James Mason as Brutus. Copyright 1953 by Metro-Goldwyn-Mayer.

wives are Linda Darnell, Ann Sothern, and Jeanne Crain, and their husbands are, respectively, Paul Douglas, Kirk Douglas, and Jeffrey Lynn.

The picture then flashes back as each wife considers her marriage and where it might have gone wrong. In doing so, Mankiewicz gives us a sly glimpse of what wives do wrong in handling their husbands.

As it turns out, it was Linda Darnell's businessman husband (Paul Douglas) that Addie had her grip on. He, however, decides that he loves his wife after all. We get the impression that the various wives intend to do better in the future—which shows definitely that this picture predates the women's liberation era. Maybe that is why it was so entertaining.

A Letter to Three Wives (1949), produced by Sol C. Siegel for Twentieth Century-Fox Film Corporation release. Directed by Joseph L. Mankiewicz. Screenplay by Mankiewicz from Vera Caspary's adaption of John Klempner's novel. Photographed by Arthur Miller. Principal cast members: Jeanne Crain, Linda Darnell, Ann Sothern, Kirk Douglas, Paul Douglas, Jeffrey Lynn, Thelma Ritter.

Joseph L. Mankiewicz made his mark in Hollywood as writer, producer, and director. Copyright 1950 by Twentieth Century-Fox Film Corporation.

1950

Joseph L. Mankiewicz for All About Eve

Although he started in Hollywood as Herman Mankiewicz's little brother, Joseph L. Mankiewicz soon proved himself one of the better screenwriters. He wrote for the likes of Josef von Sternberg, Norman Taurog, and W. S. Van Dyke before becoming a producer in 1936. He was certainly a successful producer. His credits run from Fritz Lang's *Fury* (1936) through George Cukor's *The Philadelphia Story* (1940) to John M. Stahl's *Keys of the Kingdom* (1944).

However, he had the directing bug, and, after World War II, he made his debut with *Dragonwyck* (1946). He then blazed a good commercial trail until 1949, when he gathered double Oscars for screenplay and direction of *A Letter to Three Wives*, proving himself a master of brittle, amusing dialogue. Then, just to show that this was no fluke, he took the 1950 screenplay and direction Oscars again, this time for *All About Eve*.

All About Eve was an excellent story, cast with stars like Bette Davis, Anne Baxter, George Sanders, Gary Merrill, and Marilyn Monroe in a small role. Even so, taking the best picture and director's Oscar in 1950 was no minor accomplishment. Competition was strong that year. *All About Eve* competed against such films as *Sunset Boulevard*, with Gloria Swanson, *The Third Man*, *Harvey*, *The Asphalt Jungle*, *Born Yesterday*, and *King Solomon's Mines*.

The betting was on *Sunset Boulevard* with its bravura performance by Gloria Swanson, but academy voters have their own peculiar criteria for making their choices. In this case, it may have been that they liked the idea of seeing Broadway knifed rather than their own profession.

All About Eve told the story of how a ruthlessly ambitious girl affected the lives of several people associated with the Broadway stage.

The Eve of the story (Anne Baxter) ingratiates herself with star Margo Channing (Bette Davis). She manages to get herself employed as secretary-companion to Margo, who is taken in by Eve's heavy flattery. Later, at a party for director Bill Samson (Gary Merrill), whom Margo hopes to marry, Eve is too attentive to Bill. This causes Margo to flare up. To get rid of Eve, she gets her producer (Gregory Ratoff) to give Eve a job in his office.

Margo has promised dramatic critic Addison DeWitt (George Sanders) that she will audition his protégé, Miss Casswell (Marilyn Monroe), to be Margo's understudy. She makes an appointment to read with Miss Casswell the following week. She arrives late for the audition and finds that they did not wait for her. Eve read Margo's part in her absence. Margo, furious, upbraids Lloyd Richards (Hugh Marlowe), the playwright, and director Samson. Samson walks out.

Margo's enemy, Karen Richards (Celeste Holm), arranges for Margo to miss a performance in the play. Then she and her husband, the playwright, put Eve in as understudy. Addison gives Eve a rousing review and then publishes an interview with Eve in which she makes catty remarks about aging actresses playing young-girl parts.

Margo announces her engagement to Samson and tells Richards she will not be available for his next play. Richards casts Eve instead, and she is a sensation. Returning to her hotel after her triumph, Eve finds an aspiring young actress who claims she admires Eve *so* much. This girl (Barbara Bates) is using the same pitch Eve used on Margo, but Eve is too wrapped up in her newfound fame to realize it.

The attraction of *All About Eve*, like that of *A Letter to Three Wives*, is in the brilliant dialogue that Mankiewicz wove about the framework of a good story and an exceptionally able cast.

None of Mankiewicz's subsequent pictures reached the heights of these two films. Among his later pictures were *Julius Caesar* (1953), *The Barefoot Contessa* (1954), *Guys and Dolls* (1955), *Suddenly Last Summer* (1959), *There Was a Crooked Man* (1970) and, of course, the debacle of *Cleopatra* (1963), which he took over and tried to save but couldn't.

Anne Baxter, Gary Merrill, Celeste Holm, Bette Davis, and Hugh Marlowe in Joseph L. Mankiewicz's *All About Eve*. Copyright 1950 by Twentieth Century-Fox Film Corporation.

Marlon Brando, Samuel Goldwyn, and director Joseph L. Mankiewicz on the set of *Guys and Dolls.* Copyright 1955 by Samuel Goldwyn Productions.

Joseph L. Mankiewicz uses his hands to tell Barbara Rhoads how he wants a scene played in *There Was a Crooked Man* (1970). Copyright 1970 by Warner Bros.-Seven Arts.

All About Eve (1950), produced by Darryl F. Zanuck for Twentieth Century-Fox Film Corporation release. Directed by Joseph L. Mankiewicz from a short story by Mary Orr. Photographed by Milton Krasner. Principal cast members: Bette Davis, Anne Baxter, George Sanders, Celeste Holm, Gary Merrill, Hugh Marlowe, Thelma Ritter, and Marilyn Monroe in a bit part.

George Stevens directs an outdoor scene for *The Talk of the Town* (1942). He began in films as a cameraman in 1921. Copyright 1942 by Columbia Pictures Corporation.

1951

George Stevens for A Place In The Sun

When Leo McCarey, Hal Roach, Stan Laurel, and their assorted gagmen were sitting around batting out ideas for a 1927 comedy, one of them suggested they toss a pie, for lack of a better idea. Laurel thought the gag too old, but said he would agree if they made it the most colossal pie toss in screen history. So they bought an entire pie-wagon load and pies were tossed in faces by the hundreds to make *The Battle of the Century*, a two-reel Laurel and Hardy classic.

Photographing this mammoth bit of slapstick hardly seems the kind of training that would develop a director who would someday make *Shane*, *A Place in the Sun*, and *Giant*. But that is the way it happened. George Stevens (1904–1975), two-time Oscar winner for direction, got his start as a Hal Roach cameraman. He was born in Oakland, California, in 1904, and was seventeen when he turned his back on the family profession of acting and joined Roach in 1921.

For nine years, Stevens stood behind his camera, counting "one thousand-and-one, one-thousand-and-two" and so on to time the proper cranking speed of the old silent cameras before Roach suggested that he try his hand at directing. This was in 1930, and Stevens directed two-reelers for three years. Then he moved to Universal, who gave him the feature *The Cohens and Kellys in Trouble*. This was one of the lesser achievements in a long-run Irish-Jewish series starring Charlie Murray and George Sidney.

In 1935, RKO put him on *Alice Adams*, with Katharine Hepburn as the star of the Booth Tarkington story. This was the first of Stevens' three pictures with Hepburn. The other two were *Quality Street* (1937) and *Woman of the Year* (1942). The latter began her professional and personal longtime association with Spencer Tracy.

As further evidence of his great versatility, Stevens did the Fred Astaire-Ginger Rogers musical *Swingtime* (1936), *Gunga Din* (1939), and then went back to light comedy with *The Talk of the Town*, with Ronald Colman, Jean Arthur, and Cary Grant.

World War II sent Stevens back to his original work as cameraman in the U.S. Signal Corps. At the war's end, he joined Frank Capra and William Wyler in independent production through their own Liberty Films. They would show the Cohns, Mayers, and Zukors how movies should be made. As usually happens in such cases, Liberty Films did not last long. An artist is not necessarily—in fact, rarely is—a good businessman.

Stevens produced and directed *I Remember Mama* (1948) before the company broke up. It was an excellent film, catching the spirit of an immigrant woman trying to raise a family in San Francisco. Irene Dunne was very good as Mama.

It was three years after this when Stevens was heard of again, but his comeback film was a winner, *A Place in the Sun* (1951), with Montgomery Clift, Shelley Winters, and Elizabeth Taylor. The film, which won Stevens his first Oscar for directing, was a remake of Josef Von Sternberg's 1931 *An American Tragedy*, with Sylvia Sydney and Phillip Holmes, based upon Theodore Dreiser's novel of the same name. The 1931 version was just too downbeat for audiences in the early Depression years. They had enough misery in their own lives and wanted to laugh when they went to the theater.

Jean Arthur and Cary Grant play it for laughs in Stevens's film *The Talk of the Town*. Copyright 1942 by Columbia Pictures Corporation.

I Remember Mama was the sensitive story of a Norwegian mother's struggle to raise her family in San Francisco. Irene Dunne was Mama. The two children with her here are Steve Brown and Peggy McIntire. Copyright 1948 by RKO-Radio Pictures, Incorporated.

It was Stevens' choice to remake the film under a new name, and it seemed a peculiar choice for him to make. The book was based upon an actual case that happened before World War I. A young man murdered his pregnant, lower-class girl friend in order to leave himself free to marry a girl of a higher class. Dreiser was one of the earlier liberal writers who used this case as a soap box. He was among the first to preach that it was not the criminal but society that was at fault.

Stevens opens with a long shot of a young man walking down the road. After the superimposed titles are finished, we see Angela Vickers (Elizabeth Taylor) roll past in her car. The boy, George Eastman (Montgomery Clift) looks after her hungrily, for he is a product of the slums and she represents the world of the rich that he craves.

George leaves home to work in the factory of his rich uncle. Here he learns that the beautiful Angela is his cousin. In his loneliness, he takes up with Alice (Shelley Winters), a factory girl. Alice is attracted to George and her family gradually changes its own attitude about him. With the dream of moving up in the world by marrying Angela exciting him, he is thrown into shock to learn that he has gotten Alice pregnant. He takes Alice for a boat ride and she is drowned. In his confused state, he never knows if he murdered her or not. But he is brought to trial, with Raymond Burr, foreshadowing his Perry Mason days, as the prosecutor who sends him to the electric chair.

The tragic ending did not work against the film for once, and it was justifiably one of the hits of 1951. Stevens changed the character of George, making him a more sympathetic person than he had been in either the book or the previous film. He also crowded the picture with cinematic symbolism. Due to his own long experience behind the camera, the symbolism was handled smoothly and effectively. One example is a lap dissolve from the lake to Alice's face. The overlapping of the water and the girl foreshadows her coming death in the lake. It was very effectively done, as are all of Stevens' technical operations. He views his script and cast through the double eyes of photographer and director.

After *A Place in the Sun*, Stevens made *Something to Live For* (1952) and the classic Western *Shane* (1953) before again taking the director's Oscar for *Giant* in 1956.

A Place in the Sun (1951), produced by George Stevens for Paramount Pictures Incorporated release. Directed by George Stevens. Screenplay by Michael Wilson and Harry Brown, from the novel by Theodore Dreiser. Principal cast members: Montgomery Clift, Shelley Winters, Elizabeth Taylor, Raymond Burr, Anne Revere, Freida Inescort.

If Shelley Winters and Montgomery Clift had not parked in the dark like this so often, the tragedy of her murder in *A Place in the Sun* might have been avoided. Copyright 1951 by Paramount Pictures Corporation.

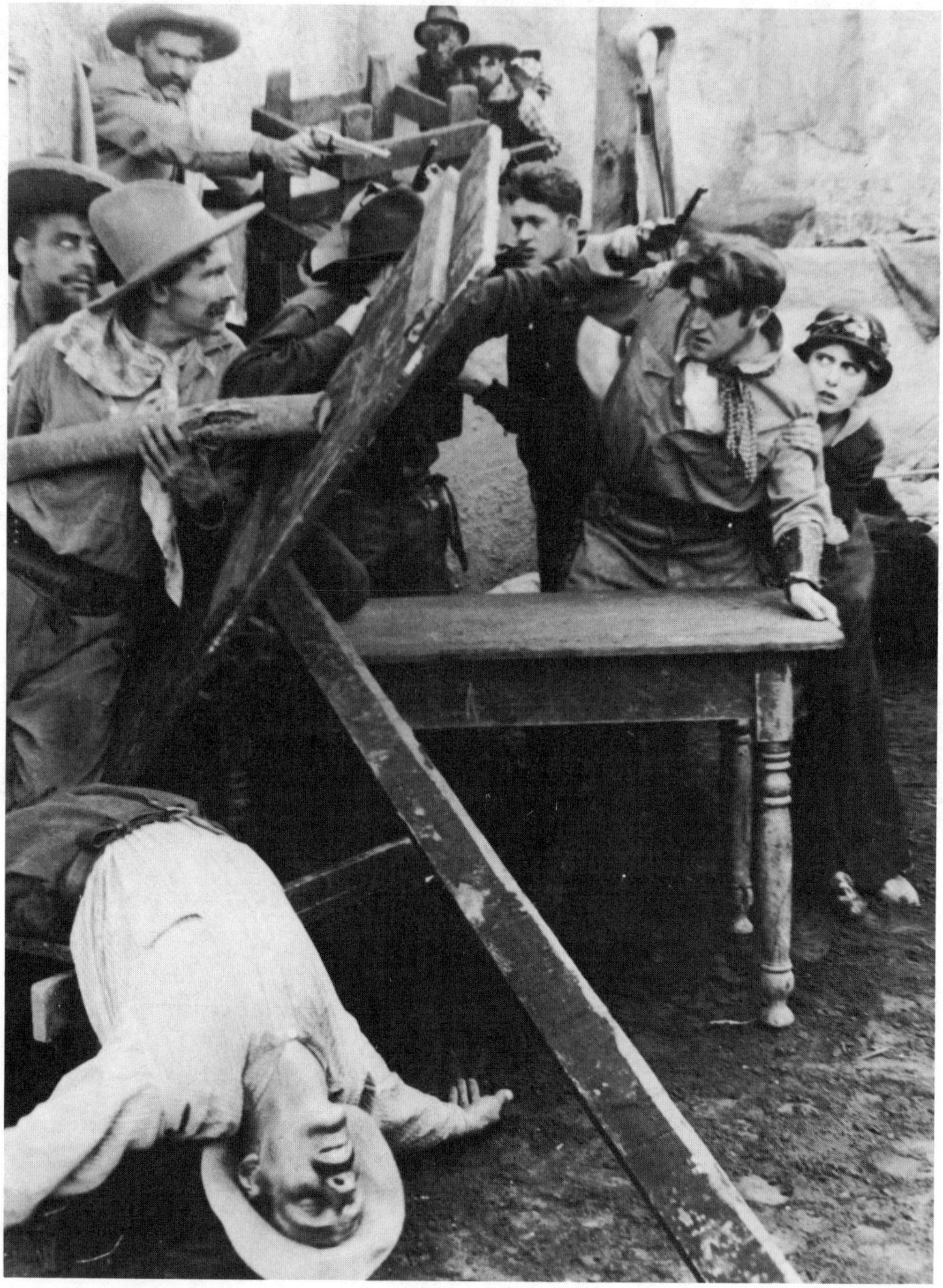

John Ford was still Jack Ford when he appeared with brother Francis and Grace Cunard in *Three Bad Men and a Girl* (1915). Jack's head appears above the arm grabbing Francis Ford's gun hand. Copyright 1915 by Universal Film Manufacturing Company.

1952

John Ford for The Quiet Man

John Ford's family came from Ireland. They pulled up their Irish roots, but John's grew deeper as he aged. Periodically, his love for the old country burst out in a picture. We see this happening in such pictures as *Mother Machree* and *Hangman's House* (both 1928), *The Informer* (1935), and *The Plough and the Stars* (1937).

It must be admitted that Ford's Irish pictures—with the exception of *The Informer*—were among the least memorable of his many films. And *The Informer* was more of a critical than a financial success.

Then came 1952 and *The Quiet Man*. This resounding success almost did not get made. One would think that any studio would have jumped at the chance of having John Ford make a film. Despite an occasional low grosser like *Flesh* (1932), Ford had done well throughout the 1930s and 1940s. In addition to his Academy Award pictures, he turned out such films as *The Hurricane* (1938), *Stagecoach* (1939), *Young Mr. Lincoln* (1939), *Drums along the Mohawk* (1939), and returned to westerns after coming back from the war.

But, despite this, studio chiefs were reluctant to back a story about a boxer who went to Ireland to forget that he had accidently killed a man in the ring. So, when Ford approached them to make a film based upon a Maurice Walsh short story called "Green Rushes," not one of the major studios would touch it.

Teaming up with Merian C. Cooper in his own Argosy Productions company, Ford got some financial backing and Herbert J. Yates of Republic Pictures put up the rest for distribution rights. Ford retitled it *The Quiet Man*. But with John Wayne, Maureen O'Hara, Barry Fitzgerald, Victor McLaglen, and the wildest fist fight since *The Spoilers* in 1914, the film was anything but quiet.

The film opens with Sean Thornton (John Wayne) being driven to his hotel by Michaeleen (Barry Fitzgerald). He sees as lovely a vision as Ireland has produced in many a long year—Mary Kate (Maureen O'Hara), to whom the technicolor camera did full justice. She turns and runs away. Fitzgerald says slyly that the girl was only a mirage caused by Sean's thirst and heads for the nearest pub.

Having accidentally killed a man in the ring, Sean has come to Ireland to forget about the tragedy. He wants to buy a cottage and has to outbid Red Will Dannaher (Victor McLaglen), brother of Mary Kate. Red Will's feelings toward Sean worsen when Sean bests him in a hand-squeezing contest that results from a handshake.

The film is replete with Irish customs, but Ford has skillfully integrated them into his film so that they are part of the plot. Deciding that Mary Kate is a desirable helpmate, he retains Michaeleen as his marriage broker. They go to see Red Will, who will have nothing to do with Sean as a brother-in-law, although Mary Kate says she will "go for the idea."

But Red Will is tricked by Michaeleen and others. They convince him that a wealthy widow he covets will not marry him as long as his sister is in the house. He agrees to the marriage, but refuses to give his sister a dowry.

Sean does not care about the lack of a dowry, but it blights the marriage for Mary Kate. So she locks Sean out of the nuptial-night bedroom. He kicks in the door, throws her on the bed, and then stalks out, having made his point that he could take her if he wished. After a while, she decides to leave. She tries to take a train for Dublin, but Sean drags her off it. He makes her walk the five miles back home, giving her a boot with his knees when she falters. They are followed by a crowd of local people who encourage him.

Instead of going home, he takes her back to Red Will, claiming she is not a fit wife because she came to him without a dowry. Will, shamed into it by the crowd, gives Sean some money which he promptly throws in a fire. This shows that he did not want the money; he merely wanted to satisfy his wife by collecting it.

Wallace Beery was a German wrestler, and Karen Morley was his faithless wife in John Ford's *Flesh* (1932). Copyright 1932 by Metro-Goldwyn-Mayer.

Francis Ford had a character role in John's 1939 film *Drums Along the Mohawk.* Copyright 1939 by Twentieth Century-Fox Film Corporation.

John Wayne had one of his better roles in *The Quiet Man* with Maureen O'Hara. Copyright 1952 by Argosy Productions.

Red Will is enraged. Sean, because of the ring tragedy, never wanted to fight again. But there is no way out now. He and Will charge each other and fight until they drop. Water is poured on them and they get up and fight some more. Sean wins, naturally—and, when he gets home this time, Mary Kate does not lock the door.

Ford put the pieces of this film together so lovingly that it was a joy to behold. Every frame rang true. Even the overly melodramatic fight seemed right and sensible.

The Quiet Man (1952), produced by Argosy Productions, for Republic Pictures Corporation release. Directed by John Ford. Screenplay from the story by Maurice Walsh. Photographed by Winton C. Hoch. Principal cast members: John Wayne, Maureen O'Hara, Barry Fitzgerald, Victor McLaglen, Ward Bond.

Fred Zinnemann won his first Oscar for *From Here to Eternity.* Portrait copyright 1966 by Columbia Pictures Corporation.

1953

Fred Zinnemann for From Here to Eternity

Fred Zinnemann wanted to be a musician. Although he had talent, he did not have that kind of talent. His family wanted him to be a lawyer. So, after considerable family argument, they compromised by permitting him to leave his native Vienna to attend a cinematographer's school in Paris.

After learning how a camera works, twenty-one-year-old Fred found a job in 1929 in the German film industry. At this time, his imagination was fired by tales he heard of Hollywood's new talking pictures. He managed to get a letter of introduction to Carl Laemmle, head of Universal Pictures. Laemmle always responded to letters from relatives or German nationals. "Uncle Carl" was born in Germany and always favored displaced Germans.

Laemmle passed the letter of introduction along to a subordinate. Since Zinnemann was not a Laemmle relative, he was lower in the job hierarchy. The best he could get was an extra assignment as a German soldier in *All Quiet on the Western Front* (1930). But, since he had been sent down by Laemmle, he was not dropped after this bit was completed. He switched uniforms and played a French soldier.

He then became assistant to director Berthold Viertel, who introduced Zinnemann to Robert Flaherty, the famous documentary-film director. Flaherty invited Zinnemann to join him on a projected Russian documentary. This was never made, and Zinnemann worked on a film with Busby Berkeley, the dance director. After this assignment, he spent a year doing a documentary in the Flaherty manner about Mexican fishermen. It was called *The Wave*, and, like most documentaries, it was more popular with critics and movie historians than with the public. But it was Zinnemann's stepping stone to the future. On the basis of this film, MGM took him into its short-subjects department.

By 1941, Zinnemann had graduated to features. The first was *The Kid Glove Killer* with Van Heflin. It was followed by the Edward Arnold vehicle *Eyes in the Night* (1942). He got his first critical success with *The Seventh Cross* (1944). Spencer Tracy starred in this anti-Nazi drama.

Not long after this success, Zinnemann was blacklisted for balking at the poor scripts MGM was trying to force on him. He made a comeback with *The Search* (1948) with Montgomery Clift and Ivan Jandl, and *Act of Violence* (1949), and hit a high standard with three pictures for Stanley Kramer, *The Men, High Noon,* and *Member of the Wedding.*

High Noon came along just when Hollywood was under fire from the House Un-American Activities Committee for Communist infiltration into movie making. Some perfectly innocent pictures were condemned as Communist propaganda, but the point of *High Noon,* which was actually intended by its

Spencer Tracy, fleeing from Nazis, pauses to rest in a German cathedral in Fred Zinnemann's *The Seventh Cross.* Copyright 1944 by Metro-Goldwyn-Mayer.

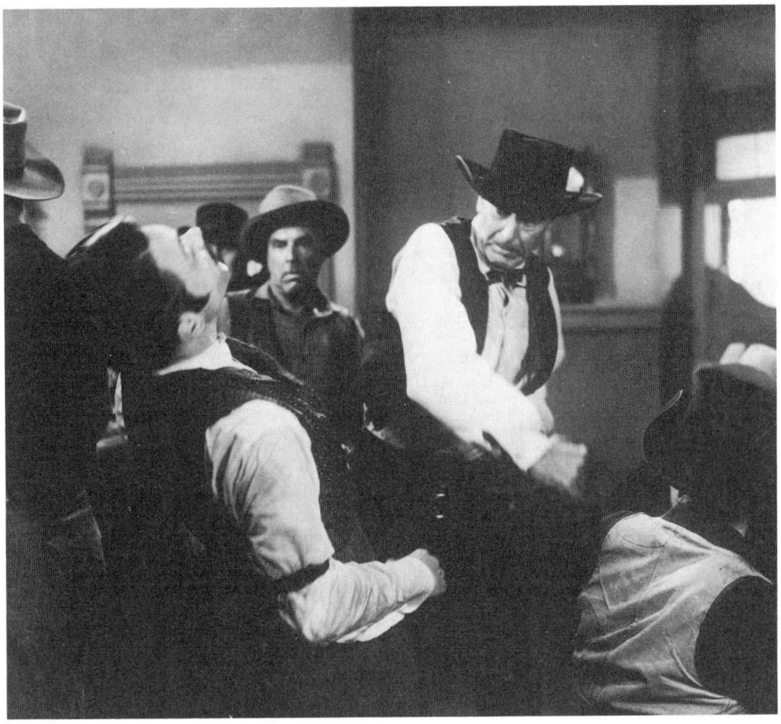

Gary Cooper, center, gave his best-remembered performance in *High Noon*. Copyright 1952 by United Artists Corporation.

writer to be such, was completely missed by both audiences and witch-hunters. None recognized it for what it was. Carl Foreman, the writer was one of those who refused to testify before the committee. He claimed later that he used the theme of a community gripped by fear to draw a parallel with what was happening in the United States. Unfortunately for Foreman's message, the public accepted it as a classic Western—which should tell us something about trying to use films for propaganda.

Then after *Member of the Wedding*, Zinnemann got his Oscar and a smash hit with *From Here to Eternity*. Sadism, brutality, adultery, and the worst features of military life were depicted against the background of "pineapple soldiering." The James Jones novel that furnished the basis for Daniel Taradash's screenplay was sprawling and disjointed. Zinnemann and Taradash tightened it into a cohesive film that expertly juggles the problems of several different people.

First, we have Private Robert E. Lee Prewitt (Montgomery Clift), an exboxer who once killed a man accidentally in a fight and does not want to box again. The captain of his company (Philip Ober) tries to force Prewitt to join the boxing squad so he can have the prestige of having a winning team under his command. Then we have the tough First Sergeant (Burt Lancaster) who is carrying on an adulterous liaison with the captain's wife (Deborah Kerr). In the background is non-conformist Maggio (Frank Sinatra), who is beaten to death in the guardhouse by a sadistic sergeant (Ernest Borgnine).

Prewitt, enraged at Maggio's death, kills the sergeant in a knife fight. At this point the Japanese attack on Pearl Harbor begins. Clift, who has been hiding in the home of Donna Reed, a prostitute's role in the book that was cleaned up for the movie, tries to get back to the base. He is shot and killed by a nervous sentry frightened by the attack.

In spite of being actually two stories in one and having a tragic ending, *From Here to Eternity* was one of the most popular films of the year. The academy membership voted it best picture and gave supporting Oscars to Sinatra and Donna Reed along with the directing award to Zinnemann.

James Jones caught the spirit of peace-time soldiering, and Zinnemann preserved a lot of it in the film. The picture was released soon enough after the end of World War II for many of the ten million exservicemen to recognize some of the truth about service life, dramatized though it was, that the picture contained.

From Here to Eternity (1953), produced by Buddy Adler for Columbia Pictures Corporation release. Directed by Fred Zinnemann. Screenplay by Daniel Taradash, from the novel by James Jones. Principal cast members: Burt Lancaster, Montgomery Clift, Frank Sinatra, Deborah Kerr, Donna Reed, Ernest Borgnine Philip Ober.

The cathouse of James Jones's novel became a more sedate "social" club in Fred Zinnemann's movie version of *From Here to Eternity.* At right are Donna Reed, Frank Sinatra, and Montgomery Clift. Copyright 1953 by Columbia Pictures Corporation.

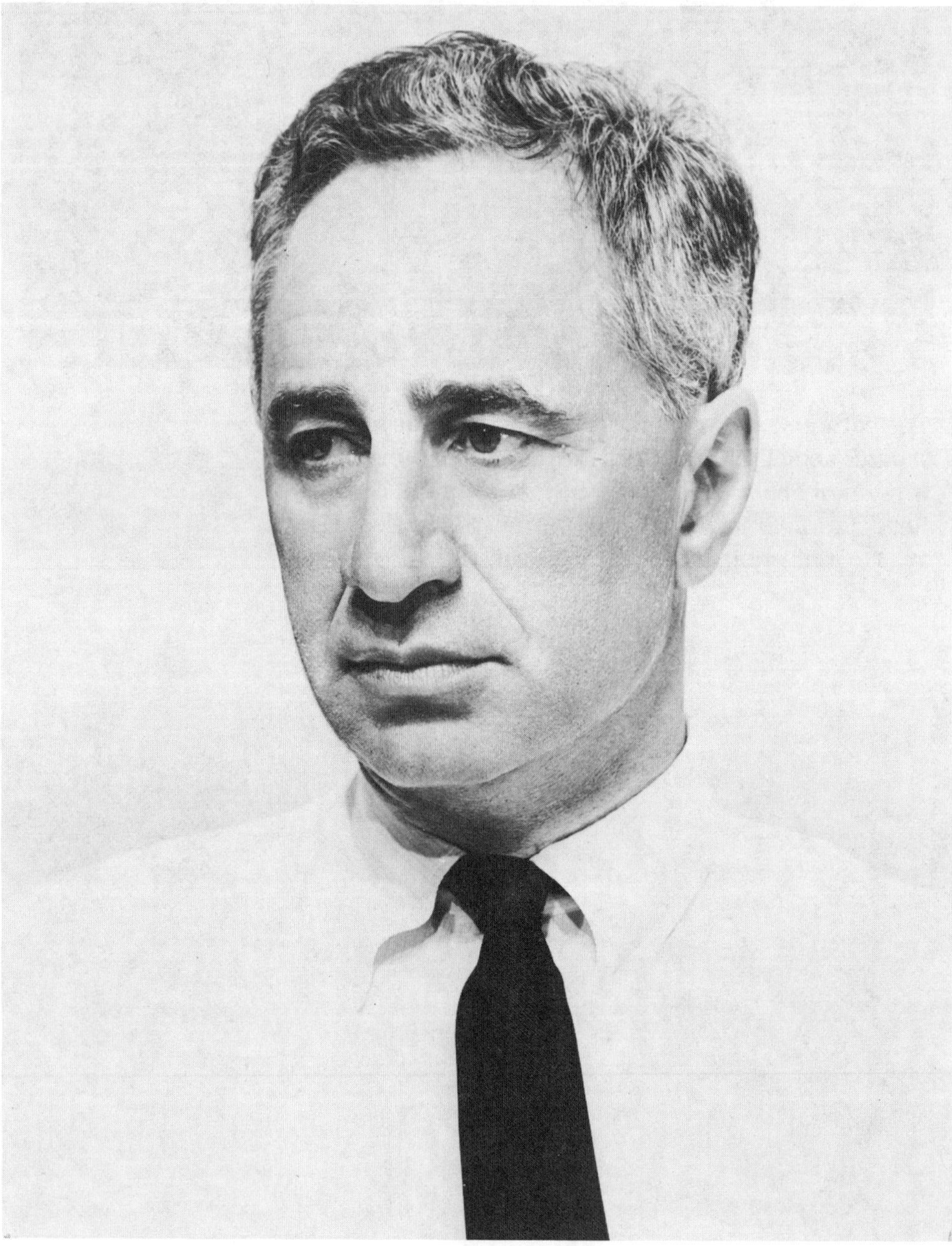

Elia Kazan, a victim of oppression in his youth, strived
to get social consciousness into his work.

1954

Elia Kazan for On the Waterfront

Elia Kazan differed from most of the ultra-liberals who tried to use show business to further their political beliefs. He kept his own mind and did not become a slave to the party. Also he differed from most of them in that he had a well developed sense of story and did not become so immersed in his "isms" that he bored us to death. One could generally depend upon Kazan for a good show—and that is a genuine novelty among those who like to make films with messages.

After *Gentleman's Agreement*, his first Oscar film, Kazan followed this mild treatment of anti-Semitism with an equally tepid treatment of black segregation in *Pinky*. John Ford started the film, which had Jeanne Crain and Ethel Waters in the cast. He withdrew after quarrels with Ethel Waters, and Kazan took over. The bland treatment in *Pinky* fitted the time. Then, after the so-so *Panic in the Streets* (1950), Kazan directed Marlon Brando in two hits, *A Streetcar Named Desire* (1952), with Vivien Leigh, and *Viva Zapata*, which was about a Mexican revolutionary. *Zapata* was Kazan's first film after he testified before the House Un-American Activities Committee, an act that infuriated his liberal friends and made them his enemies.

Although Kazan turned his back on the American Communist Party, he retained his basically Communist views. His gentle treatment of Zapata, who was hardly the heroic figure the film made him out to be, showed this.

Then came *On the Waterfront* and a second Oscar. The academy also gave the film the best picture award. Brando took the acting honors, and Eva Marie Saint was judged the best supporting actress.

Budd Schulberg wrote the story, with heavy assistance from Kazan, basing it upon factual articles by Malcolm Johnson of the New York *Sun*.

Terry Malloy (Brando) is a flunky for a racketeering union boss who leads him to set up a union member for murder. The murdered man is the brother of Edie Doyle (Eva Marie Saint), who wants revenge. She and Terry had known each other as children and now meet again. She does not know he was involved in her brother's death and begs him to help her. Through her and a militant waterfront priest (Karl Malden), Terry comes to realize the rottenness of the union chief (Lee J. Cobb).

Terry's brother (Rod Steiger) is a crooked lawyer working for the union. He is sent to warn Terry, and then is killed when he fails to keep Terry quiet. In a powerful scene showing the confrontation between the two brothers, the alienation between them and the bitterness of the past and present all come out. This scene was highly regarded by all critics.

Terry rejects the traditional "deaf-and-dumb" code and testifies before a crime commission. He is ostracized by the union and prevented from working. Taking the law into his own hands, he goes to the union office and reasserts his rights by beating up the union chief.

The ending is ridiculously unrealistic, the only flaw in what, up to this time, had been a brilliant film.

After *On the Waterfront*, he made *East of Eden* (1955), with James Dean, and Julie Harris, *Baby Doll* (1956), with Carroll Baker, Karl Malden, and Eli Wallach, *A Face in the Crowd* (1957), with Andy Williams, and *Wild River* (1960), with Montgomery Clift and Lee Remick. All were exceptional pictures.

Next came *Splendor in the Grass* (1961), with Natalie Wood and Warren Beatty. This was followed by *America America* (1963), based upon his own novel. It dealt with the problems of Anatolian Greek immigrants to the United States. Kazan then waited six years before he made another film, *The Arrangement*. Again, he worked from his own novel, which had been a best seller.

His final picture was *The Visitors*, which was simply a labor of love. It was shot in super-sixteen-millimeter in the manner of a bunch of amateurs trying to break into the industry. Apparently, he had a lot of enjoyment making it and got his $135,000 cost.

Marlon Brando was Terry Malloy in Elia Kazan's *On the Waterfront*. Copyright 1954 by Columbia Pictures Corporation.

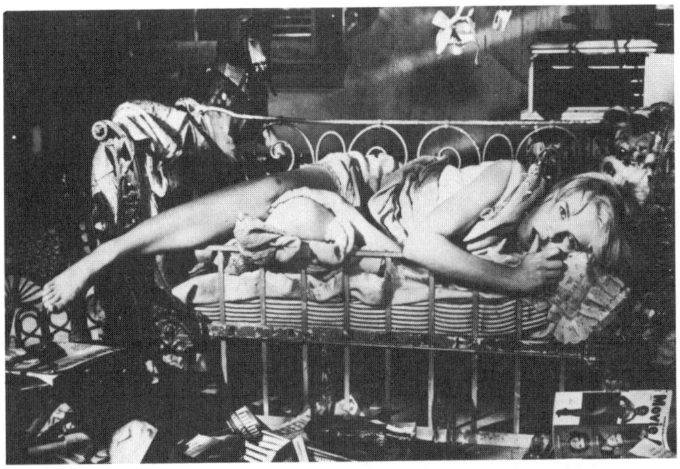

Baby Doll was Kazan's interpretation of Tennessee Williams' tale of love and infidelity in the deep South. Carroll Baker was the overripe girl-bride. Copyright 1957 by Warner Brothers Productions.

Joan Blondell was the aunt, and Ted Donaldson and Peggy Ann Garner were the children in Kazan's first film, *A Tree Grows in Brooklyn*. Copyright 1943 by Twentieth Century-Fox Film Corporation.

Kazan made only eighteen pictures over a period of twenty-six years, beginning with *A Tree Grows in Brooklyn* (1943). He also kept up his stage direction. While he sometime slipped, like every other director, in the main his record is outstanding.

On the Waterfront (1954), produced by Sam Spiegel for Columbia Pictures Corporation release. Directed by Elia Kazan. Screenplay by Budd Schulberg, based upon a series of newspaper articles by Malcolm Johnson. Principal cast members: Marlon Brando, Eva Marie Saint, Karl Malden, Lee J. Cobb, Rod Steiger.

Delbert Mann was the first TV director to make a success in theatrical films. Copyright 1965 by Metro-Goldwyn-Mayer.

1955

Delbert Mann for Marty

The 1955 Academy Awards indicated that the unsuspecting movie industry had let a fox into its chicken yard.

This was a time when movie attendance was abysmal, and producers were blaming the tube rather than the extremely poor pictures they had been making. Television was, therefore, the prime enemy of the motion picture industry, even more perfidious than the censor, previously the number one villain. The bad guys, in violation of movie tradition, were apparently winning.

Then a shocking thing happened. When they voted for *Marty* as the best picture of 1955, the Academy members supported the enemy by handing out Oscars to a television director making his first theatrical film. To make the situation worse, *Marty* was a remake of a popular TV presentation, and the author, Paddy Chayefsky, was primarily a TV writer. Faced with a situation like this, movietown old-timers could well suspect that the black hats from television were going to take over the whole show.

Fortunately for the good guys, directors like Delbert Mann and stories like *Marty* did not sprout in every TV studio. Delbert Martin Mann, Jr. (b. 1920), the first television director to shift to motion pictures, came from a non-theatrical family by way of Lawrence, Kansas.

Mann was active in high school dramatics and followed this up at Vanderbilt University and the Community Theater, Nashville. He joined the U.S. Air Force in 1941 and became a bomber pilot, flying combat with the Eighth Air Force in Europe. After the war, he attended the Yale School of Drama. He was with stock companies until joining NBC as an assistant director in 1949. Later, as a director, he directed 100 hour-long shows from 1949 through 1955. *Marty*, from a script by Paddy Chayefsky, was one of these. According to tradition, Harold Hecht and Burt Lancaster only produced the screen version through their independent company to have a loss as a tax write-off on their more profitable production.

If this is true, they got badly fooled, for *Marty* proved a highly profitable sleeper. The story line pretty much followed the TV play, except that the lonely, fat, Jewish butcher became a lonely, fat, Italian butcher. Marty (Ernest Borgnine), a very good butcher, is thirty-five years old and totally unsuccessful with girls. This dismays his mother (Esther Minciotti), who wants him married. We follow Marty through his associations with his buddies—looking at girlie books, talking about how great Mickey Spillane's blood-and-sadism novels are—we see their attempts to pick up girls.

They go to a dance hall where a friend, stuck with an unattractive blind date (Betsy Blair), offers Marty ten dollars to take her off his hands. Marty refuses, but shortly after sees the girl, Clara, rushing from the hall. He follows her and tries to cheer her up. In their talk, the two lonely people are drawn to each other.

Opposition arises. Marty's friends tell him that Clara is a "dog." Mama, who was so anxious for him to marry and produce grandchildren, now is very much against the girl because she is not Italian.

Ernest Borgnine gave an outstanding performance as the lonely butcher caught in the struggle between his own desires and the claims of family and friends that he can do better than Clara. Against this background of opposition, Marty must work out his own destiny.

"All I know," he says, "is that I'm happy when I'm with her." At this point, he rejects those who called Clara a "dog." He calls her for a second date. When she agrees, he goes out to the street. Unable to express his happiness in words, he slams his fist against a Stop sign.

All successful pictures are products of their time. Many of them, if made earlier or later, might not have been so successful. Nearly a quarter of a century has passed since *Marty* was made. Then, it filled the theaters while movie producers were crying doom, but the picture does not carry the punch today that it did then, for we are different people from those who enjoyed *Marty*.

Ernest Borgnine was *Marty*, a very good butcher who finally found himself a girl friend in a film voted the best by the Academy membership in 1955. Copyright 1955 by United Artists Corporation.

Mann's third film was Eugene O'Neill's *Desire under the Elms,* with Sophia Loren and Anthony Perkins. Copyright 1957 by Paramount Pictures and Don Hartman Productions.

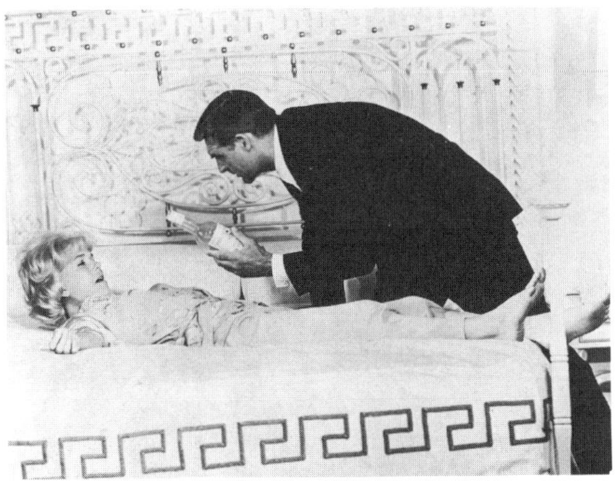

That Touch of Mink is a far cry from *Marty.* It was a farce comedy with Doris Day and Cary Grant. Copyright 1962 by Universal Pictures Corporation.

There is not a lot to be said for it technically. It was hastily made, owing more to TV techniques than to film. However, a lot of people have been lonely, and they felt good to see one of their kind break out of his shell. Both men and women could find someone to identify with, and they packed the theaters to do it.

After *Marty,* Mann went on to make such films as *Desire under the Elms* (1958), *The Dark at the Top of the Stairs* (1960), *That Touch of Mink* (1962), *Mister Buddwing* (1966), and others.

Marty, (1955), produced by Hecht-Lancaster for United Artists Corporation release. Directed by Delbert Mann. Screenplay by Paddy Chayefsky, from his original Playhouse 90 TV-script. Photographed by Joseph LaShelle. Principal cast members: Ernest Borgnine, Betsy Blair, Esther Minciotti, Joe Mantell.

George Stevens studies the script for *Giant,* a story of changing values in the Texas ranch country. Copyright 1956 by Warner Brothers Pictures Corporation.

1956

George Stevens for Giant

George Stevens, like most of the old timers who began in silent pictures, liked to have his way. These veterans believed strongly that they knew better than actor, writer or studio bosses how pictures should be made. Stevens was not shy in letting this be known, as a TV network found out when it tried to cut one of his pictures to fit a time slot.

When one looks back on his record, it appears that he may have known better than most how to make pictures. There was *Woman of the Year* (1942) which brought Katharine Hepburn and Spencer Tracy together for the first time, *A Place in the Sun* (1952), his first Oscar film, the memorable *Shane* (1953), and *The Greatest Story Ever Told* (1965), among others. *The Diary of Anne Frank* (1959) was not so well received, but this was rare indeed with George Stevens.

Stevens believed with Shakespeare that "the play's the thing." His major interest was always the story. Actors, lighting, and camera were simply tools to help him tell his tale in pictures. With this attitude, it is difficult to see what Stevens had in mind when he selected James Dean, a surly, moody, and not-too-cooperative method actor to play one of the major roles in *Giant*. Dean had been seen in but one film, *East of Eden*, when Stevens selected him for the part of Jett Rink. Dean had made one other picture, *Rebel Without a Cause*, but it had not yet been released. It was enough, however, to impress Jack Warner of Warner Brothers that he had a big star in the making.

Dean's natural surliness just fitted the character Stevens had in mind. The picture got made, even though Dean thought Stevens was a lousy director and Stevens thought Dean was a deliberately uncooperative actor. At one point, Stevens took him up to Jack Warner for discipline.

Despite these troubles, *Giant* was a success and earned Stevens his second Oscar for directing. No one more richly deserved an award. It was Stevens' film all the way. He had to take a sprawling Edna Ferber novel and squeeze it down to size without appearing to confine it. It was his idea to make the film in the first place, and he had to make a deal to bring in author Ferber on a percentage to get her to agree. Then Stevens had a script written by Fred Gilland and Ivan Moffat, which he polished and fiddled with for two years before taking the package to Jack Warner for financing.

Warner readily agreed. Why not? With Elizabeth Taylor, Rock Hudson, plus upcoming star James Dean, and with Stevens's hit record, how could he lose? Especially with an Edna Ferber story. Wasn't Miss Ferber the author of *So Big*, *Show Boat*, *Old Man Minick* (a play), *Cimarron*, *Come and Get It*, and *Saratoga Trunk*, in addition to being co-author of *Dinner at Eight* and *The Royal Family of Broadway?* The woman apparently couldn't write a money loser if she tried.

Giant deals with changing values against a background of Texas ranching and oil. Bick Benedict (Rock Hudson) brings Leslie, his Virginia bride (Elizabeth Taylor), to his sprawling West Texas ranch. She is soon disillusioned. Luz (Mercedes McCambridge), Bick's sister, disapproves of the marriage, which she shows by trying to set up separate rooms for the newlyweds. But Luz, who has been running the ranch, is soon killed after being thrown from her horse. Luz, who never married, surprises them all by leaving ten acres of the ranch to Jett

Max von Sydow made a magnificent Christ in Stevens' *The Greatest Story Ever Told* (1965). This scene shows Christ entering Jerusalem on Palm Sunday. Copyright 1965 by United Artists Corporation.

Millie Perkins had the title role in Stevens's *The Diary of Anne Frank* (1959). Copyright 1959 by Twentieth Century-Fox Film Corporation.

Elizabeth Taylor and James Dean both were excellent in *Giant*, for which George Stevens won his second director's Oscar. Copyright 1956 by Warner Brothers Pictures Corporation.

Rink (James Dean), a surly ranch hand who would have long since been fired except for Luz. Jett hates Bick and has a crush on lovely Leslie. He resists all efforts to get him to sell his inheritance, and builds a shack on his land.

One day, Leslie stops by on her way back from helping some Mexican children. As she is leaving, she gets her shoe dirty in what Jett recognizes as oil seeping up from the ground. He manages to finance a drilling rig and becomes fabulously oil-rich.

They all age, and we see Jett—now thoroughly obnoxious—trying to regain his lost youth by pursuing Bick and Leslie's young daughter (Carroll Baker) and finally dieing after making a speech at a banquet.

The acting was above average, winning Oscar nominations for both Rock Hudson and James Dean. Both lost to Yul Brynner in *The King and I.* Elizabeth Taylor showed that she had more than just beauty to offer. And Stevens made very good use of the new wide screen to graphically bring out the immensity of the land and its effect upon the characters.

Giant (1956), produced by George Stevens and Henry Ginsberg for Warner Brothers Picture Corporation release. Directed by George Stevens. Screenplay by Fred Gilland and Ivan Moffat, from the novel by Edna Ferber. Principal cast members: Rock Hudson, Elizabeth Taylor, James Dean, Mercedes McCambridge, Carroll Baker, Sal Mineo, Jane Withers, Chill Wills, Dennis Hopper.

David Lean, director of *The Bridge on the River Kwai,* makes few pictures, but he has a genius for making the unbelievable believable. Copyright 1957 by Columbia Pictures Corporation.

1957

David Lean
for The Bridge on the River Kwai

A long time ago, there was a satirical song that informed us that, at the proper time, in Britain "everything stops for tea." This is not overexaggerated, and David Lean can be grateful for it. It got him into films, as a teenage tea-server to the cast of a British film.

In time, Lean (b.1908), became an assistant cameraman and then settled back as an assistant editor. He began on newsreels and progressed to feature films. He liked editing. His work as a cameraman aided his work. Editing is much more than just splicing together the day's rushes. Many mediocre directors have been saved by the tempo that a skillful editor put into their plodding work.

Lean developed quite a reputation as a "cutter." One of his notable achievements was the editing of *Pygmalion* (1938), with Leslie Howard and Wendy Hiller in the roles later played by Rex Harrison and Audrey Hepburn when Bernard Shaw's play became the musical film *My Fair Lady.*

Lean had several times been offered a picture to direct, but had always refused. Then came the war, and Noel Coward asked him to assist in directing *In Which We Serve.* This was a semi-fictional tribute to Lord Louis Montbatten, who had lost a ship he commanded in the battle of Crete. Lean handled the action sequences for Coward, who both directed and starred as the ship's commander.

The picture was a success, and Coward was pleased enough with Lean's work to let him direct three Coward stories, *This Happy Breed* (1944), about war on the home front; *Blithe Spirit* (1945), in which a dead wife returns to harrass her remarried husband; and *Brief Encounter* (1945), about a short affair between two married people. Then, from Coward, Lean turned to Dickens, making an excellent *Great Expectations* (1946) and a superior *Oliver Twist* (1948). In the next nine years, he made five more pictures, including *Hobson's Choice,* with Charles Laughton. This was an excellent picture with Charles Laughton giving a superior performance as the father who did not want to lose his daughters to marriage. It was not, however, the kind of picture to draw big American audiences.

Then came 1957 and *The Bridge on the River Kwai.* This film proves that, if the director and star are adroit enough, the public will suspend its disbelief and swallow the most ridiculous story. It was written by Pierre Boulle from his novel, *The Bridge over the River Kwai*, a satire on the old-school type of British army officer. The satire was dropped for the film, and Boulle was induced to add an American, William Holden, as a concession to U.S. audiences. This should have ruined it, but, by some miraculous chemistry between director and cast, the film came out a gripping, suspenseful, and entertaining film. The academy membership thought enough of it to present Oscars for best film, best actor, and best direction.

In the movie, Sessue Hayakawa, a veteran going back to the days of Thomas H. Ince, is Colonel Saito, commander of a Japanese-run prison camp charged with building a military railroad-bridge in western Thailand. Colonel Nicholson (Alec Guinness) is the senior British officer among the prisoners. He flatly refuses to permit his officers to work on the bridge. He stoically undergoes torture until Colonel Saito compromises: the British officers will not have to work if they will act as advisors.

Nicholson agrees. In his mania, he puts out superhuman efforts to build the bridge. He must show the enemy his British superiority. In the meantime, the American, Shears (William Holden), escapes and joins forces with a British commando (Jack Hawkins) to destroy the strategic bridge. Nicholson discovers the dynamite charges and reports to Saito, "Someone is trying to blowup my bridge."

In the ensuing melee, the American is killed. This brings Nicholson to a realization of what he has done to aid the enemy. He destroys the bridge himself. At this point, a very effective scene shows the wreckage of the bridge spread across the wide screen. It is awesome indeed. Then the camera zooms back, and we see the wreckage as a speck in the jungle.

Jean Simmons, Martita Hunt, and Anthony Wager in David Lean's picturization of *Great Expectations*. Copyright 1946 by Universal Pictures Corporation.

Charles Laughton in *Hobson's Choice* did not want to disturb his comfort by permitting his daughters to marry. The daughters are Prunella Scales, Brenda de Banzie, and Daphne Anderson. Copyright 1954 by United Artists Corporation.

Alec Guinness and Sessue Hayakawa confront each other in David Lean's *The Bridge on the River Kwai.* Copyright 1957 renewed 1974 by Columbia Pictures Industries, Inc.

Ordinarily, this would be poor story-telling. After all the hullabaloo and suspense, it is irritating to learn that this was an infinitesimal matter to the jungle and probably to the war effort. In this case, however, it seemed exactly right. Anyway, both critics and audiences loved it. Even the theme tune, whistled by the prisoners as they marched off to work, became a hit as *The Colonel Bogey March.*

The Bridge on the River Kwai (1957) produced by Sam Spiegel. Released by Columbia Pictures Corporation. Directed by David Lean. Screenplay by Pierre Boulle, based upon his own novel. Photographed by Jack Hildyard. Principal cast members: Alec Guinness, Sessue Hayakawa, Jack Hawkins, William Holden.

Vincente Minnelli (right) with producer Martin Ransohoff, producer, during the filming of *The Sandpiper*. Copyright 1965 by MGM-Filmways.

1958

Vincente Minnelli for Gigi

When Judy Garland, in *A Star is Born*, sang that she was "born in a trunk," she might well have been talking about her exhusband Vincente Minnelli (b. 1913). For it was in Chicago that Vincente Minnelli, Sr., one of the partners in The Minnelli Brothers Big Dramatic Company, became a father while on tour. He was assisted, of course, by his French wife, Nina LeBeau, who was also the company's leading lady.

The Minnellis' show was a traveling company that performed under a tent throughout the midwest. In such a show, everyone had to pitch in. So young Vincente became an actor at the age of three. For the next five years, he played whatever child parts the repertoire required. Actor Minnelli became a has-been at eight years old. He was a victim of vaudeville and the movies. People no longer went to tent shows.

Having come from one profession famous for letting its people go hungry, Minnelli turned toward another equally well-known for letting its people starve in a garret. He decided to become an artist. He worked first for a sign painter when he was thirteen and later spent a short time at the Chicago Art Institute.

He was first a window-dresser for a department store and then a photographer's assistant before talking Balaban and Katz, the Chicago theater chain, into letting him be a set designer. He did well, and, when Paramount-Publix bought out Balaban and Katz, Minnelli transferred his talents to the Paramount Theater in New York. Later, he spent several years designing sets, costumes, and staging presentations at Radio City Music Hall. Then, in 1935, he directed a full stage-musical, *At Home Abroad*, for the Shubert brothers. Other shows followed, and Hollywood beckoned. Paramount took him to the West Coast for eight months and then let him go. He came back to Broadway and staged the Jerome Kern musical *Very Warm for May* in 1939.

Another Hollywood offer tempted him back west. This came from Arthur Freed, the legendary producer of MGM musicals. Freed himself had been a song writer, best remembered today for *Singing in the Rain*. He was also a member of the team that produced the songs for *Broadway Melody* in 1929.

Freed saw Minnelli as the man to carry on MGM's glossy musical tradition, but he was careful to give his protégé a two-year apprenticeship before turning him loose on a film. During this time, Minnelli was a glorified flunky. He read scripts, wrote scripts, designed sets, and did anything else he was asked to do. One chore led to his later marriage. He directed Judy Garland in her solo numbers for *Babes on Broadway*, the Busby Berkeley 1941 release.

After this, Arthur Freed decided Minnelli was ready and handed him an all-black musical called *Cabin in the Sky*. The story seems to have taken ideas from both Ferenc Molnar's *Liliom* and Marc Connolly's *Green Pastures*. Joe (Eddie "Rochester" Anderson) has a nightmare in which he is killed and is about to be taken to hell. Petunia's (Ethel Waters) prayers convince God to give Joe six months back on earth to redeem his soul. If he can do so, he will be received in heaven. If not, then Lucifer, Jr., can have him. Joe wins, naturally, despite being sidetracked by Lena Horne.

Margaret O'Brien and Judy Garland do the cakewalk to the music of Tom Drake's mandolin in *Meet Me in St. Louis*, which Minnelli directed in 1945. Copyright 1945 by Metro-Goldwyn-Mayer.

Leslie Caron in *Gigi* is bored by the attempts of Isobel Jeans and Hermione Gingold to make her into a desirable candidate for a rich man's mistress. Copyright 1958 by Metro-Goldwyn-Mayer.

Cabin in the Sky was amusing, but notable mainly for its splendid cast. In addition to Anderson, Waters, and Horne, it had Louis Armstrong, Duke Ellington's orchestra, and the Hall Johnson Choir.

This was followed by Red Skelton in *I Dood It*, about which a lot need not be said, but his third venture was a solid hit. It was Judy Garland in *Meet Me in St. Louis*. Judy singing the *Trolley Song* alone was worth the price of admission. In this picture, Minnelli demonstrated his genius for integrating musical numbers into a story.

In the next fourteen years, Minnelli turned out eighteen pictures and parts of two others. *Father of the Bride* and *An American in Paris* were among them. Then came *Gigi* and a director's Oscar for Minnelli.

Gigi can be summed up in one word—delightful. From the novel by the famous French writer Colette, *Gigi* is the story of a young girl raised by her grandmother (Hermione Gingold) and aunt (Isobel Jeans). Having been quite successful courtesans who never married, they feel it their duty to provide for little Gigi (Leslie Caron) by establishing her as the mistress of wealthy young Gaston (Louis Jourdan). Also, all their efforts are for naught, for, while they work to make Gigi Gaston's mistress, the young lady adroitly leads him to the altar.

Such a plot outline does not do justice to the wonderful interplay of characterization, integration of music and story, perfection of dialogue, and use of just the right settings to point up the story. Minnelli put everything he had learned, from tent show to Broadway to Hollywood, into this film. Aided by a perfect cast, he turned out a picture that audiences found a joy to behold.

Gigi took eight Academy Awards. In addition to Minnelli's director's Oscar, it was voted best picture, screenplay, color photography, art direction, costume design, scoring, and editing. Maurice Chevalier also got a special award, honoring his long years in films. His role of the charming boulevardier in *Gigi* recalled him to attention. *Thank Heaven for Little Girls*, his solo from *Gigi*, became the musical trademark for his later years, just as *Louise*, from his 1929 debut film, *Innocents of Paris*, had been the theme song of his earlier years.

Gigi (1958), produced by Arthur Freed for Metro-Goldwyn-Mayer release. Directed by Vincente Minnelli. Screenplay and lyrics by Alan Jay Lerner and Frederick Loewe, from the short novel by Colette. Photography by Joseph Ruttenberg. Principal cast members: Leslie Caron, Maurice Chevalier, Louis Jourdan, Hermione Gingold, Isabel Jeans, Eva Gabor.

"I Remember it well," sings Maurice Chevalier to Hermione Gingold as they recall an old romance. Copyright 1958 by Metro-Goldwyn-Mayer.

William Wyler won his third Oscar for *Ben Hur*, the third filming of the famous story by General Lew Wallace. Copyright 1959 by Metro-Goldwyn-Mayer.

1959

William Wyler for Ben Hur

Before shooting the chariot race in *Ben Hur*—one of the most famous scenes of stage and screen—director William Wyler made a little speech. He pointed out that he had been one of the numerous assistant directors on the 1926 silent version of the film, one of the classics of the screen. Now he wondered which of his own assistant directors would someday film a later version of the famous story by General Lew Wallace.

Directing *Ben Hur*, which had been fabulously successful as a book, a stage play, and a silent film, should have been a delight for any director. But Wyler, who had been directing for thirty-three years and was twice an Oscar winner, turned it down. Sam Zimbalist, the producer, persisted. He rejected Wyler's complaint that *Ben Hur* was for the likes of Cecil B. DeMille. He said he wanted a director who could keep the intimate feeling of the human story and not let it get lost in the spectacle. Wyler still insisted that spectacle was not his bag. Perhaps he was recalling the trials Charles Brabin and later Fred Niblo had with the silent *Ben Hur*. But he was worn down, for which he should be everlastingly grateful to Zimbalist.

Wyler did keep his eye on the characters, and they did not get lost in the mighty spectacle of battles, mammoth sets, and a chariot race—staged by Yakima Canutt and Andrew Marton—that will probably never be surpassed in any future remake.

In doing the screenplay, scripter Karl Tunberg stuck to the story line, for how could anyone dare depart from such a well known story? Judah Ben Hur (Charlton Heston), a rich Jewish prince in Jerusalem, is sentenced to a lifetime as a galley slave after an accident injures a Roman governor. His boyhood friend Messala (Stephen Boyd), a Roman, could have aided him, but chose to betray Ben Hur. While a galley slave, Ben Hur is shipwrecked during a sea battle. He manages to save himself and the Roman commander Arrius (Jack Hawkins). He is freed and adopted by Arrius. Later, Ben Hur drives Shiek Ildrem's (Hugh Griffith) horses in the chariot race against his old enemy, Messala. Messala is killed trying to wreck Ben Hur's chariot. Ben Hur then sets out to find his mother and sweetheart, who have become lepers. They are cleansed by Christ on His way to Golgotha.

Wyler did a spectacular job himself in weaving together the human story and the great spectacles. This was certainly not an *auteur* film. It took a legion of experts to make this kind of film, but Wyler deserves outstanding credit for the way he wove all their efforts together into a film so highly regarded that it brought more academy Awards for a single picture than any other in the history of the Oscars. It earned eleven—for best picture, actor, direction, supporting actor, cinematography, art direction, sound recording, musical scoring, editing, special effects, and costume designs. It missed best actress. Haya Harareet from Israel was lovely enough, but the role of Esther has always been a nonentity. Esther is in the story just for window dressing. She has absolutely nothing to do except to provide Ben Hur with the obligatory girl friend. Actresses from the Klaw and Erlinger stage production to May McAvoy in the 1926 film have complained of how little Esther had to do.

Besides his other Academy Award films, *Mrs. Miniver* (1942) and *The Best Years of Our Lives* (1946), Wyler's films included: *These Three* (1936), *Wuthering Heights* (1939), *The Heiress* (1949), *Roman Holiday* (1953), *The Children's Hour* (1962), and *Funny Girl* (1968).

Stuntman Joe Canutt is thrown into a handstand in a spectacular wreck during the filming of *Ben Hur*. Copyright 1959 by Metro-Goldwyn-Mayer.

Geraldine Fitzgerald, David Niven, Merle Oberon, and Laurence Olivier were in Wyler's *Wuthering Heights*. Copyright 1939 by Samuel Goldwyn Productions.

The 1962 remake of *These Three* under its stage title of *The Children's Hour*, with Audrey Hepburn and Shirley MacLaine, fell short of the original. Copyright 1962 by United Artists Associated.

Ben Hur (1959), produced by Sam Zimbalist for Metro-Goldwyn-Mayer release. Directed by William Wyler. Screenplay by Karl Tunberg, from the novel by General Lew Wallace. Photographed by Robert L. Surtees. Principal cast members: Charlton Heston, Stephen Boyd, Jack Hawkins, Haya Harareet, Hugh Griffith, Martha Scott, Sam Jaffe.

Billy Wilder demonstrates how a bed should be made for *The Fortune Cookie*. Copyright 1966 by United Artists Corporation.

1960

Billy Wilder for The Apartment

After the huge success of *Sunset Boulevard* (1950), the writing team of Charles Brackett and Billy Wilder broke up. It was Wilder's idea. He never gave a reason for it, and Brackett professed not to know. However, other sources have claimed that it was due to Wilder's ego. He thought that Brackett was getting too much credit for their joint successes.

Whatever the reason, Wilder's first film after the breakup was the biggest flop of his career. It was called *Ace in the Hole* (1951) and was about a callused newspaper man played by Kirk Douglas who was willing to let a man die to make a good story. The film was recalled and re-released as *The Big Carnival*, but the new title was no help.

This jolt caused Wilder to abandon messages and turn back to comedy. First came *Stalag 17* (1953), with William Holden, followed by *Sabrina* (1954), with Audrey Hepburn and Humphrey Bogart, and *The Seven Year Itch* (1955), with Tom Ewell doing the itching for Marilyn Monroe. Then, abandoning comedy, he took on the disastrous *Spirit of St. Louis* (1957), with James Stewart as Charles A. Lindbergh. This was followed by *Love in the Afternoon* (1957). While better than the boring Lindbergh biography, it was hardly Gary Cooper's best picture or even his medium-best. But *Witness for the Prosecution* (1959) put Wyler back on top again, drawing excellent performances from Marlene Dietrich, Charles Laughton, Elsa Lanchester, and Tyrone Power in the best play ingenious Agatha Christie ever wrote.

Then, in *Some Like It Hot* (1959), set-dictator Wilder met his match in don't-give-a-damn Marilyn Monroe. Despite this, an amusing picture resulted from this story of two fugitive musicians disguised in drag taking refuge in an all-girl band. However, Wilder is quoted as saying he was too old and too rich to go through another picture with Monroe.

But while Marilyn soured his disposition, she did nothing to his sardonic sense of humor, which was in fine form for his next film. This was *The Apartment* (1960), which brought him his second director's Oscar and was a milestone in the career of Jack Lemmon.

The Apartment is based on the premise that sex is the best way to get ahead in business. C. C. Baxter (Jack Lemmon) does not have the basic qualifications for success, being neither a luscious blond, a gigolo, or a pretty boy. So, to get ahead, he starts loaning his apartment to philandering bosses. This often forces him to sleep in the park, but he is immediately tagged as the executive type and begins advancing in the company.

The elevator operator in his office building is Fran Kubelik (Shirley MacLaine), upon whom our hero has designs. Unfortunately, she happens to be the one that Baxter's big boss, Sheldrake (Fred MacMurray), takes to Baxter's apartment. Returning after one such room loan, Baxter finds that Fran has taken an overdose of sleeping pills because Sheldrake will not divorce his wife to marry her. He calls Dr. Dreyfuss (Jack Kruschen) for help. Dreyfuss thinks Baxter is the cause of her attempted suicide. She recovers with Baxter's help, and Sheldrake's wife divorces him. He wants Fran back, but Baxter finally asserts himself, tells off his boss, quits, and he and Fran go off to live happily ever after.

Shirley MacLaine was the only decent character in the film, being, as the old expression goes, "more sinned against than sinning." The rest, despite Lemmon's last-reel change, were all slobs. But they were such amusing slobs that we can hardly fault the academy membership for voting Wilder the director's Oscar.

MacLaine and Lemmon made an excellent team and were back for an encore in *Irma La Douce*, which Wilder directed in 1963.

Kirk Douglas was the newspaperman in *The Big Carnival*, the retitled *Ace in the Hole*. Copyright 1950 by Paramount Pictures Corporation.

Jack Lemmon and Jack Kruschen try to revive Shirley MacLaine, who has taken too many sleeping pills in *The Apartment*. Copyright 1960 by United Artists Corporation.

Shirley MacLaine was also in Wilder's *Irma La Douce*. Copyright 1963 by United Artists Corporation.

The Apartment (1960), United Artists Corporation release. Produced and directed by Billy Wilder. Screenplay by Billy Wilder and I.A.L. Diamond. Photographed by Joseph LaShelle. Principal cast members: Jack Lemmon, Shirley MacLaine, Fred MacMurray, Jack Kruschen.

Robert Wise checks a scene during the filming of *Two for the Seesaw*, the picture that followed his Oscar-winning *West Side Story*. Copyright 1962 by the Mirisch Company, Incorporated.

1961

Robert Wise for West Side Story

The films directed by Robert Wise (b. 1914) began with *The Curse of the Cat People* (1944). They go through such edifying titles as *The Body Snatcher* (1945), *Blood on the Moon* (1948), *Something for the Birds* (1952), and then into films like Paul Newman in *Somebody up There Likes Me* (1956), and the tear-laden *I Want to Live* (1958), among others.

Curses, horrors, bloody fisticuffs, and weeping women hardly seem the basic qualifications for directing a musical, but Wise did it in *West Side Story* (1961), and then repeated in *Sound of Music* (1965). He won a director's Oscar for both of them.

Wise, who was born in Indiana, left home in the Depression year of 1933 to join his brother, an accountant at RKO, in Hollywood. He ended up in the shipping department. This brought him into contact with editors, for whom he carried cans of film. Before long, he had become an apprentice cutter himself. He worked at first on sound tracks, and then became an assistant editor. Like David Lean in England, he was learning how movies were assembled by pasting scenes together and working with directors and producers. As an editor, he worked on Orson Welles's *Citizen Kane* and *The Magnificent Ambersons*, among others.

West Side Story, which gave Wise his first director's Oscar, started as a Broadway musical inspired, so it was said, by *Romeo and Juliet*. The Montague-Capulet feud became rivalry between two youth gangs, and the star-crossed lovers were affiliated with the different gangs. In the story, Maria (Natalie Wood) is a new arrival from Puerto Rico. Her brother Bernardo (George Chakiris) is leader of the Sharks, who are deadly rivals of the Jets. Maria falls in love with Tony (Richard Beymer), a member of the Jets. Their association causes a rumble between the two gangs. Maria begs Tony to try to stop the fighting. Before he can do anything, Riff (Russ Tamblyn), leader of the Jets is stabbed by Bernardo. In a fury at the killing of his friend, Tony grabs up a knife and stabs Bernardo. Horrified at what he has done, he goes to beg forgiveness of Maria for killing her brother. He asks her to run away with him. Before they can leave, the vengeful Sharks arrive and Tony is killed. Maria weeps over his body, as the two gangs, sobered by the triple killings, put aside their enmity to carry Tony's body away.

***The Curse of the Cat People* was Robert Wise's first directorial assignment. Simone Simon and young Ann Carter were in the cast. Copyright 1944 by RKO-Radio Pictures, Incorporated.**

A stage production is confined to the stage on which it is presented. The first requirement for transforming a stage play into a movie is to "open it up;" that is, to take advantage of the camera's ability to move beyond the confines of a stage. This, Wise did to perfection in *West Side Story*. It is a special tribute to his ability that he was able to weld the violent, often abstract, choreography of Jerome Robbins into the realism of his sets and produce an artistic entity instead of a jarring hybrid.

The academy voters recognized the technical superiority of the film, giving it ten Oscars, pushing *Ben Hur*'s record eleven. George Chakiris as Bernardo and Rita Moreno as his fiery girlfriend, Anita, both took supporting actor and actress awards. In addition, the film won the best picture, best direction, and technical awards. The only critical sour note was the general opinion that Richard Beymer was a little too passive to play the part of Tony. Natalie Wood, in only her second mature role after leaving child parts behind, did very well in the role of Maria.

West Side Story (1961), produced by the Mirisch Company for United Artists Corporation release. Directed by Robert Wise. Screenplay by Ernest Lehman. Choreography by Jerome Robbins, who is also credited as co-director. Photographed by Daniel L. Fapp. Principal cast members: Natalie Wood, Richard Beymer, George Chakiris, Rita Moreno, Russ Tamblyn.

I Want to Live! was Robert Wise's picturization of the true story of a girl who was electrocuted for her part in a brutal murder. Copyright 1958 by United Artists Corporation.

The balcony scene from *West Side Story* featured Natalie Wood and Richard Beymer, recasting Shakespeare's lovers in terms of tenement rumbles and street gangs. Copyright 1961 by the Mirisch Company, Incorporated.

David Lean goes over the script of *Dr. Zhivago* with Geraldine Chaplin. Copyright 1966 by Metro-Goldwyn-Mayer.

1962

David Lean
for Lawrence of Arabia

David Lean has never shown much regard for haste in making motion pictures. Since he gave up editing to become Noel Coward's assistant on *In Which We Serve* (1942), Lean directed only eleven films in the fifteen years up to and including *The Bridge on the River Kwai* (1957).

After winning an Oscar for *Kwai*, he waited five years before presenting his next film, *Lawrence of Arabia*. Usually, when a director is off the screen for five years, it means that nobody asked him to work. This was hardly the case with Lean. After the unusual financial success of *The Bridge on the River Kwai*, he was inundated with scripts. None of them interested him. After his previous success, he felt he had to expand. He could not afford to make a lesser film. He wanted something of epic proportion, and was willing to wait until he got it. It turned out to be a long wait. Word was whispered around that he had quit.

But finally he found what he wanted, and his long delay was justified, for the film was another Oscar winner, taking the top picture award and bringing Lean his second award for best directing. The film was *Lawrence of Arabia*. It took best picture, best direction, best color photography, best color art direction, best scoring, and best editing. Although Peter O'Toole got a nomination for best actor in the title role, he lost to Gregory Peck in *To Kill a Mockingbird*.

T.E. Lawrence, the subject of this film biography, was one of those enigmatical people who turn into legends. Their real character gets lost in myths, and, forever after, people speculate on what they were really like. Americans first heard of Lawrence through Lowell Thomas's book, *With Lawrence in Arabia*. Later, Lawrence wrote his own account of his adventures in *Seven Pillars of Wisdom*, which was the basis of Robert Bolt's screenplay for the film.

Lawrence was an archeologist, working in the Middle East. When World War I started, he went into the British Intelligence service. His specific assignment was to organize the Arab tribes to fight the Turks who opposed the British in this area. He was extraordinarily successful. This was due partly to his charismatic leadership and partly to the Arabs' belief that they were fighting for their independence. After the war, the British government repudiated the promises

Alec Guinness, Omar Sharif, and Peter O'Toole, in *Lawrence of Arabia*, in the crucial meeting that brought Arabs and British together in the war against the Turks. Copyright 1962 by Columbia Pictures Corporation.

Lawrence made to the Arabs and took control of the Palestine and Jordanian regions under a League of Nations mandate. Lawrence, embittered by the rejection, resigned his commission and enlisted in the army as a private soldier. He was killed in a motorcycle crash in 1935.

Sam Spiegel bought the rights to Lawrence's story in 1960, but filming did not begin until 1961. Lean took a long time to dig thoroughly into the life of Lawrence. He wanted to understand the man as well as he could before he began shooting. As the script finally took shape, it dealt primarily with Lawrence as a bigger-than-life leader. Lean opened with the motorcycle death of Lawrence (Peter O'Toole) in 1935 and then flashed back to the war. In the film, Lawrence contacts Prince Faysal (Alec Guinness) and obtains fifty men. Then, in association with Sharif Ali (Omar Sharif), Lawrence makes a dramatic march through the desert. Here he persuades another sheikh (Anthony Quinn) to join him in an attack on a Turkish outpost. The small band is extraordinarily successful, mainly because Lawrence gained the respect of the Arabs. The photography and composition of the figures in the setting provide a remarkable feeling of desert emptiness, and we can feel the heat, loneliness, and excessive harshness of this bitter environment. In the human side of the story, Lawrence begins to emerge as a megalomaniac with a touch of sadism in his nature.

He returns to Cairo and is sent back again to organize guerrilla raids. These peak when General Allenby sends him to spearhead an attack on Damascus in Syria. Here, Lawrence's growing bloodthirstiness climaxes as he urges his men into a massacre. He orders no quarter and no prisoners. Every one of the enemy is to be slaughtered.

After this, Arab fractionalism and (not shown) British refusal to make good on Lawrence's promises begins to undo the coalition Lawrence put together. He withdraws.

Although Lean likes to quote Noel Coward about how much a writer or director should know about a character, Lean deals only with Lawrence the warrior. The enormously complex character of this tortured man does not come out in the picture. This leaves us wondering about some of his actions. As shown, *Lawrence of Arabia* is a mammoth story of adventure and war. After its first showing, the picture was cut. The re-release was definitely hampered by these omissions. This shows how well Lean cuts his films. As an ex-editor, he works closely with his official editors, and the resulting picture is his. Anything that comes out after he gets done with it weakens one of his films.

After *Lawrence of Arabia*, Lean waited four more years and then produced another epic, *Dr. Zhivago* (1966).

Lawrence of Arabia (1962), produced by Horizon Pictures for Columbia Pictures Corporation. Directed by David Lean. Screenplay by Robert Bolt, based upon material in *Seven Pillars of Wisdom* by T.E. Lawrence. Photographed by F.A. Young. Principal cast members: Peter O'Toole, Alec Guinness, Anthony Quinn, Omar Sharif.

Filming a scene in *Dr. Zhivago*, Lean's next film after *Lawrence of Arabia*. Copyright 1966 by Metro-Goldwyn-Mayer.

Tony Richardson came on strong in his first films, but faded quickly.

1963

Tony Richardson for Tom Jones

When Squire Alworthy (George Devine) found a bastard baby in his house, he adopted the child and called it Tom Jones. Then, in silent-film subtitle style, the movie tells us "—of whom the opinion of all was that he was born to be hanged."

Such an engaging chap could not help but interest audiences, and *Tom Jones* became the hit of 1963. It was based upon Henry Fielding's novel of the progress of an eighteenth-century rake from bed to bed. Albert Finney played Tom exactly as Fielding wrote him.

The director of *Tom Jones* was lauded as highly as the film and his cast, receiving the year's Oscar for directing. Unfortunately, *Tom Jones* proved the peak in Tony Richardson's (b. 1928) directorial career. Richardson bloomed quickly and faded just as fast. He was born the son of a pharmacist. He was a film fan as far back as he can remember, spending every hour he could in the theaters. Then, when he was twelve, Richardson directed a school play and his career ideals were set.

He went into TV and met playwright John Osborne, whose play *Look Back in Anger* Richardson later directed. After the success of this play, he and Osborne formed their own company, filming Osborne's *The Entertainer*, with Laurence Olivier.

Richardson was noted for contemporary realism, and *Tom Jones* was a startling departure for him. After the teaser opening, we find Tom as a wenching young man who is not particular about the type or class of his women just as long as they are lusty. Turned out of the house after the squire can take no more, Tom leaves his local loves behind and sets out for London, moving from bed to bed, and almost getting hanged in the process. In the end, in true romantic fashion, we find that his mother was highborn after all. Tom comes into his inheritance and gets the girl—although we feel he would have done better with the earlier Diane Cilento, a Moonbeam McSwinish type.

Reviewers like the *New York Times's* Bosley Crowther lauded the film's cinematic tricks. These included the whole bag: freeze frames, suspended action, asides to the audience, and coy actions like Tom's putting his hat over the door knob to cut out the audience's view of what was to go on in the bedroom.

Laurence Olivier starred in *The Entertainer*, Tony Richardson's second film. Copyright 1960 by Continental Distributing Corporation.

When an author or director is telling a story, all elements should contribute to suspending our disbelief for the duration of the story and causing us to believe that this is really happening. When an actor turns to the audience and asks, "Did *you* see her take that £500?", then the director or writer is jarringly reminding us that this is only a film anyway.

A frozen frame may be dramatic, but it is not real. A collection of cinematic tricks recalls Mack Sennett, who never tried to be anything but ridiculous anyway. The trouble with cinematic tricks is that they call attention to themselves. A story should be a totally integrated whole. Anytime a trick, scene, actor, or anything else in a film calls attention to itself, then that film is less than perfect. The purpose of a story is to tell a story or make a point. We must—temporarily, anyway—believe in it. This is hard to do when the director or his befuddled editor keeps reminding us that it is only a film. In a correctly made film, all parts will blend into one satisfying whole.

However, the bawdy sexiness, the splendid acting by perfectly cast performers, the good story, and believable sets made *Tom Jones* a financial success. Tony Richardson seemed headed for the top, but something happened. His next film, *The Loved Ones* (1964), was as bad as *Tom Jones* was good. Piqued by criticism, he grew sullen and irritated the press. He tried such tricks as stationing two guards to keep reporters off his set. Naturally, this led to still worse press that was not helped by the quality of the films he turned out, such as *Mademoiselle* (1965), *The Charge of the Light Brigade* (1968), and *Ned Kelly* (1970).

Tom Jones (1963), produced by Tony Richardson for United Artists Corporation release. Directed by Tony Richardson. Screenplay by John Osborne, from the novel by Henry Fielding. Photographed by Walter Lassally. Principal cast members: Albert Finney, Susannah York, Hugh Griffith, Edith Evans, Joan Greenwood, Diane Cilento.

Albert Finney, seen here with Susannah York, made a marvelous *Tom Jones*. Copyright 1963 by United Artists Corporation.

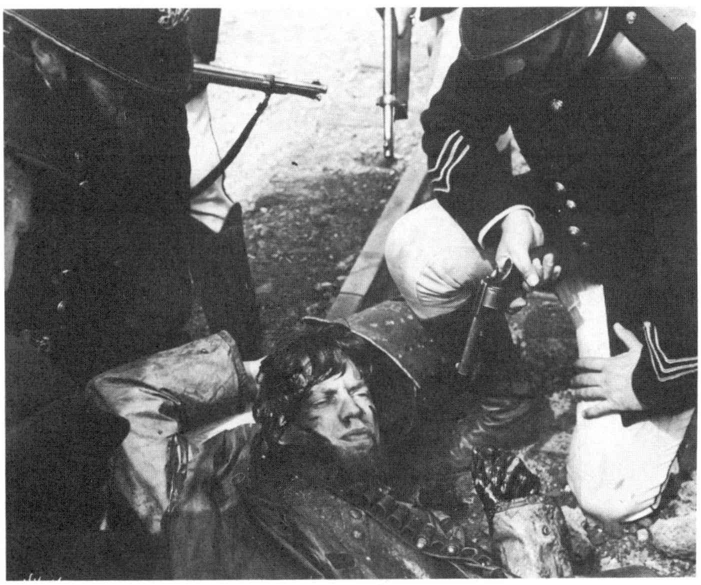

Mick Jagger had the title role in Richardson's *Ned Kelly*, the story of an Australian outlaw. Copyright 1970 by United Artists Corporation.

George Cukor directs Audrey Hepburn in the opening sequence of *My Fair Lady*. Copyright 1964 by Warner Brothers Pictures Corporation.

1964

George Cukor for My Fair Lady

When George Cukor (b. 1899) won the director's Oscar in 1964 for *My Fair Lady,* a lot of us thought, "Well, it's about time!" As we look back on the almost fifty films that Cukor has made since he came to Hollywood in 1929, we realize that his pictures may not be as good as we thought at the time, but they were often better than those that did win Oscars in the same years.

This was certainly exemplified in 1937, when *The Life of Emile Zola* took the best picture award, Leo McCarey got the director's award for *The Awful Truth,* and Luise Rainer was named best actress for *The Good Earth.* It was also the year that Cukor made *Camille,* with Greta Garbo at her peak.

On the other hand, Cukor also directed Garbo in *Two-Faced Woman* (1941), which is probably her worst film. However, in between these two extremes, he has such notable achievements as *A Bill of Divorcement* (1932), in which Katharine Hepburn made her screen debut; *Dinner at Eight* (1933), in which Jean Harlow and Wallace Beery outshone a brilliant all-star cast; *David Copperfield* (1935) with Freddie Bartholomew; *The Women* (1939); *Gaslight* (1944); *A Double Life* (1947), which brought a star's Oscar to Ronald Colman; *Born Yesterday* (1950); *A Star Is Born* (1954); and *Les Girls* (1957). There were many others, including *Let's Make Love* (1960), which we can just forget, and *Romeo and Juliet* (1936), also forgettable.

Then came *My Fair Lady* (1964) and an Oscar at last, after thirty-four years of trying.

Cukor, now in his eighties, was born in New York City. He started in the theater in 1919 as a stage manager in the Chicago company of *The Better 'Ole,* a World War I comedy based upon a famous cartoon. A cockney soldier in a shellhole in France with bombs bursting all around tells his grousing companion, "If you know a better 'ole, go to it!"

After some years in Rochester working in stock, he went to New York in 1925. Four years later, he was in the group of Broadway directors frantically summoned to Hollywood to help make the transition from silence to noise. He was dialogue director for Paramount's *River of Romance* with Wallace Beery,

Mary Brian, and Buddy Rogers, and did the same chore for *All Quiet on the Western Front* at Universal. He came back to Paramount and was credited as codirector on *Grumpy* (1930), with Cyril Maude.

After a couple of other assists, he was given full director's credit on *Tarnished Lady* (1931), with Tallulah Bankhead.

My Fair Lady, which finally brought him his Oscar, is the musical adaptation of George Bernard Shaw's *Pygmalion*. In Greek mythology, Pygmalion was an artist who fell in love with a statue, Galatea, he had carved. Zeus pitied him and brought the lovely lady to life. In Shaw's play, and in the musical version with Shaw's words and music by Alan Jay Lerner and Frederick Loewe, Galatea becomes Eliza Doolittle, an illiterate Cockney flower girl, and Pygmalion is phonetics professor Henry Higgins.

Higgins (Rex Harrison), amused at Eliza's (Audrey Hepburn) atrocious speech, tells his friend Pickering (Wilfred Hyde-White) that in three months he could pass the girl off as a duchess simply by teaching her to talk like one.

Eliza is willing to learn, for she hopes that improved speech will enable her to get a job as a clerk. The three work hard—and we in the audience were the winners as they set elocution lessons to music in the delightful "Rain in Spain" sequence. They decide that Eliza is ready and take her to the races at Ascot. She

Freddie Bartholomew was *David Copperfield*, and W.C. Fields was Mr. Micawber in Cukor's picturization of the Dickens novel. Copyright 1935 by Metro-Goldwyn-Mayer.

Ronald Colman won an Oscar as best actor of the year in George Cukor's *A Double Life*. Copyright 1947 by Universal Pictures Corporation.

Reginald Denny, John Barrymore, Leslie Howard, and Basil Rathbone in *Romeo and Juliet* (1936), Cukor's less-than-successful foray into Shakespeare. Copyright 1936 by Metro-Goldwyn-Mayer.

isn't quite finished, but does well enough for Pickering and Higgins to congratulate themselves. Eliza is hurt because they fail to recognize her part in it all.

She leaves and it is then that Higgins realizes that "I Have Grown Accustomed to Her Face." Higgins's mother advises Eliza not to return until he asks her. He does.

George Bernard Shaw was one of the great playwrights of his time. As such, he presumably had a message in his play. In the transfer to the screen, any message in *My Fair Lady* was thankfully lost, leaving just plain fun.

My Fair Lady (1964), produced by Jack L. Warner for Warner Brothers Incorporated release. Directed by George Cukor. Screenplay by Alan Jay Lerner, from the Lerner and Loewe stage production and George Bernard Shaw's play *Pygmalion*. Photographed by Harry Stradling. Principal cast members: Audrey Hepburn, Rex Harrison, Wilfred Hyde-White, Gladys George.

Robert Wise coaxes a smile from Kym Karath, who plays the youngest Von Trapp child in *The Sound of Music.* Copyright 1965 by Twentieth Century-Fox Film Corporation.

1965

Robert Wise
for The Sound of Music

Writers who are not directors themselves often have harsh things to say about the way directors and producers mutilate their work. The classic case, of course, is F. Scott Fitzgerald's plaintive moan, "Can't producers ever be wrong?"

Robert Wise, as a producer-director, is not among these. From the days when he made films like *The Body Snatcher* (1945) through *Somebody up There Likes Me* (1956) to his Academy Award film *West Side Story* (1961), Wise's writers all speak of the freedom he gave them. Later he picks and chooses, but in the beginning he asks for all the ideas they have. He does not interfere until the script is completed, in contrast to many directors who are looking over the writer's shoulder at every line.

In an interview once, Wise said that he even encouraged his writers to put down their suggestions for cutting. When he does review their work, he never rewrites. He just makes suggestions for changes he thinks are necessary. He does not work for a tight script that is almost a cutting script, as men like John Ford did. Wise likes to have plenty of film, an attitude that goes back to his own days as an editor. He knows from experience the value of having some extra frames if a hole develops.

After the success of *West Side Story*, Wise did not do so well with *Two for the Seesaw* (1962), with Shirley MacLaine and Robert Mitchum, and *The Haunting* (1963), but he was back in Academy Award style with *The Sound of Music* (1965), a picturization of the successful Richard Rodgers and Oscar Hammerstein Broadway play. In addition to Rodgers' and Hammerstein's music, *The Sound of Music* had a book by Howard Lindsay and Russell Crouse, the authors of the long-running *Life with Father*. Someone said that having these four on a property was like having the national treasury underwriting the production's finances.

The involves Maria (Julie Andrews), a novitiate in a nunnery who is such a tomboy that the abbess wonders if she really should be a nun. She sends Maria to be governess for the seven children of widowed Baron von Trapp. Maria has some initial difficulty with the children, but wins them over. While the baron is away, she teaches them to sing. They do so well that they want to enter in the singing at the Salzburg Festival. The baron (Christopher Plummer) returns and refuses to permit it. Maria quarrels with him and returns to the abbey. The abbess realizes that Maria has fallen in love with the baron and sends her back to resume her work as governess. The baron also realizes that he missed Maria while she was gone. They marry just as World War II begins.

The Baron, who abhors Naziism, is ordered into the military service. The entire family tries to escape, but is stopped by German storm troopers. They are allowed to proceed after convincing the commandant that they are going to the Salzburg Festival to let the children compete in the singing contest. After the contest, they hide in the abbey and then make their escape across the border.

The film was made on location in Salzburg, Austria, and introduced Julie Andrews to the screen. While many critics thought the film less than inspired, they all agreed that Julie was superb. When award time rolled around, the Academy voters disagreed with the critics on the picture and gave it the Oscar as the year's best, along with another Oscar for director Wise. About all that can really be said for the film is that it was a sweetly sentimental tale told engagingly with a minimum of stickiness. It was genuine fun to watch. It was also a real money-maker.

But apparently neither star nor director is as important as a likeable—though not necessarily good—story. The same director and star failed to click in *Star!*, a screen-biography of Gertrude Lawrence, filmed in 1968.

Boris Karloff and Russell Wade were in Robert Wise's early horror film, *The Body Snatcher*. Copyright 1945 by RKO-Radio Pictures, Incorporated.

Paul Newman and Pier Angeli were in Wise's *Somebody Up There Likes Me.* Copyright 1956 by Metro-Goldwyn-Mayer.

Julie Andrews and the seven children were responsible for much of *The Sound of Music*'s charm. Copyright 1965 by Twentieth Century-Fox Film Corporation.

The Sound of Music (1965), produced by Robert Wise for Twentieth Century-Fox Film Corporation release. Directed by Robert Wise. Screenplay by Richard Lehman, from the stage musical by Richard Rodgers, Oscar Hammerstein, Howard Lindsay, and Russell Crouse. Photographed by Ted McCord. Principal cast members: Julie Andrews, Christopher Plummer, Eleanor Parker, Peggy Wood, plus a gaggle of children.

Anthony Franciosa and Fred Zinnemann check the script during filming of *A Hatful of Rain* (1957). Copyright 1957 by Twentieth Century-Fox Film Corporation.

1966

Fred Zinnemann for A Man for All Seasons

Fred Zinnemann is an example of the auteur type of director. He wants to say something in his film, and he wants—insists, in fact—in saying it in his own way. However, it was only after the enormously successful *From Here to Eternity* and *High Noon* that he was able to gain complete artistic control. Producers reasoned that any director as smart as this could be left alone.

But, as often happens when successful directors are left alone after having producers like Stanley Kramer riding check on them, Zinnemann on his own did not do as well as Zinnemann under Kramer. He made *A Hatful of Rain* (1957), about the struggle of an ex-serviceman to kick the drug habit; *Sundown* (1960), with Robert Mitchum and Deborah Kerr in the story of an Australian drifter; and the disastrous *Behold a Pale Horse* (1963), which put Gregory Peck in the Spanish Civil War. Suddenly Zinnemann was no longer regarded as one of the top five Hollywood directors.

Then came *A Man for All Seasons* (1966) to restore his tarnished reputation and to bring him a second Oscar for directing the best picture of the year. At least, it was the best in the eyes of the academy voters.

A Man for All Seasons began as a very successful London play by Robert Bolt. Paul Scofield, the star, scored a personal triumph, which he repeated with equal success in the Broadway production. Scofield played Sir Thomas More, the historical character who had to choose between his God and his king.

Bolt had been trying since 1960 to get a movie company interested in the play. Finally, through William Graf, Columbia Pictures' London representative, he got Columbia's Mike Frankovitch interested. He took the project to Zinnemann, but Columbia put on a strict $2 million budget-ceiling. Most of those involved believed in the film so much that they agreed to cut their usual prices. Zinnemann filmed in England, with an English cast, using local castles and homes to further reduce costs.

Paul Scofield repeated his stage role of Sir Thomas More, who was appointed Chancellor of England by Henry VIII. Henry (Robert Shaw) is intent upon divorcing Queen Catharine of Aragon in order to marry Anne Boleyn (Vanessa Redgrave). The Pope refuses to sanction the divorce, and More is caught in the struggle between the Pope and Henry. Henry forces an act through Parliament creating the Church of England with the king as spiritual leader as well as the political head of England.

More resigns. His enemies see this as a chance to destroy him. They claim that his silence is actually a rebuke to the king, although More openly refrained from any criticism of Henry's actions. They demand that More swear allegiance to Henry as the spiritual head of the country. More refuses and is imprisoned. Further accusations are raised against him. He is accused of treason and is sent to the block.

Columbia thought *A Man for All Seasons* an artistic, prestige film and fervently hoped that it would at least break even. It was hardly a subject that would appeal to a mass audience. However, it took six Academy Awards, including best picture, best actor, and best director. This insured its financial success, greatly surprising and pleasing the Columbia brass. For Zinnemann, it was a moment of triumph after a troublesome barren period.

Zinnemann did a good job on *The Sundowners* with Robert Mitchum, Deborah Kerr, and (in background) Michael Anderson, Jr., but the story of an itinerant family in Australia was too downbeat for the public. Copyright 1960 by Warner Brothers Productions.

Arthur Franz, Nancy Gates, and Julie Harris in the early Zinnemann film *Member of the Wedding*. Copyright 1953 by Columbia Pictures Corporation.

Susannah York, Paul Scofield, and Wendy Hiller in Zinnemann's Oscar-winning *A Man for All Seasons*. Copyright 1966 by Columbia Pictures Corporation.

A Man for All Seasons (1966), produced by Fred Zinnemann for Columbia Pictures Corporation release. Directed by Fred Zinnemann. Screenplay by Robert Bolt, from his play of the same name. Photographed by Ted Moore. Principal cast members: Paul Scofield, Wendy Hiller, Susannah York, Robert Shaw, Leo McKern, Vanessa Redgrave, and Orson Welles in a brief role as Cardinal Wolsey, More's predecessor.

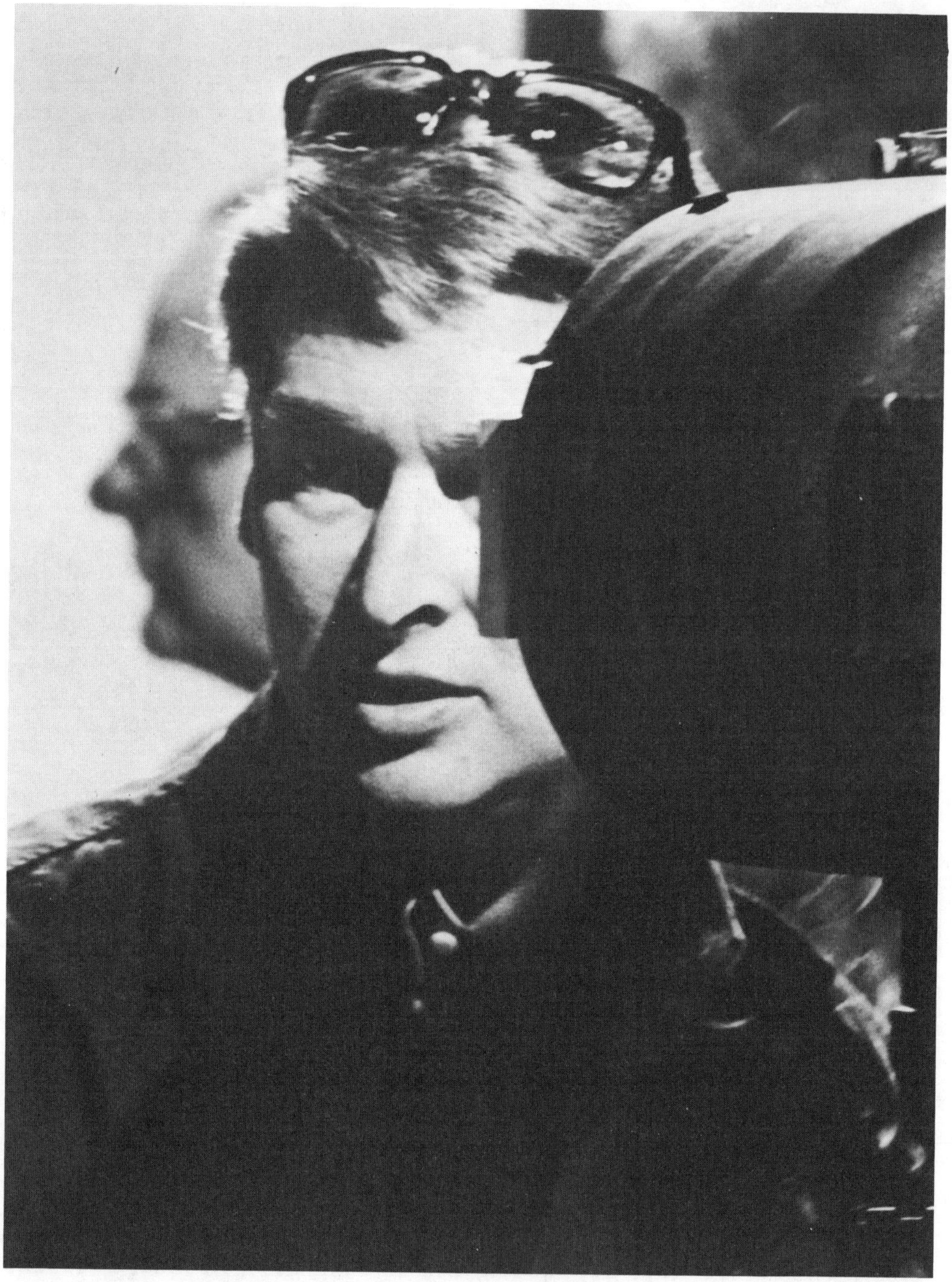

Mike Nichols directing *The Graduate*, the film that brought him an Academy Award. Copyright 1967 by Embassy Pictures Corporation.

1967

Mike Nichols
for The Graduate

Shakespeare's observation about the rose and its smell makes us wonder if a Mike by any other name would make movies as sweet? What brought this up is that a Mike once named Peschkowsky, but who now goes under the name of Nichols, is on record as regretting that his father changed the family name upon immigrating to the United States.

"Michael Igor Peschkowsky, isn't that a marvelous name?" the present Mr. Nichols asks.

But he must lack the courage of his beliefs, since it would take little legal trouble to change it back to Michael Igor etc. After all, there is movie precedent for name swapping. A Mr. S. Spiegel first became S. P. Eagle and then decided he preferred being himself.

Nichols (b. 1931) is a triple-threat man if ever there was one. As a performer, he was a nationally known comedian. As a director, he received the 1967 Academy Award for *The Graduate,* a film that brought accolades from men like Wyler and others among the top director ranks. Then, as a Broadway producer, he receives the credit "Mike Nichols presents" for *Annie,* the brightest Broadway hit of many a year. When the show is finally filmed, we can be sure that Mike Nichols' name will be prominently attached to that also.

Nichols was born in Berlin, Germany, on 6 November. His father, a doctor, had fled to Germany to escape persecution in Russia. The family lived in Germany until 1939, when they immigrated to the United States. By 1954, Nichols entered the University of Chicago, ending up in amateur campus musicals. He is on record as saying this was not a result of an abiding love for the theater. He thought he might meet girls more easily this way. Among those he met was Elaine May. They drifted together and ended up as a team. The teaming was professional only, apparently, for each has married several times, but they have never married each other.

They went to New York with thirty dollars in cash to storm the big town, and worked their way into night clubs. This brought them to TV, and they developed a national reputation as a comedy team. Hedda Hopper, the columnist, said of them, "They brought a new kind of laughter to the U.S."

Then Nichols was given the opportunity to direct a play out in the sticks. He liked it so well that he accepted the director's position for *Barefoot in the Park* (1963), which was quickly followed by *Luv* (1964), *The Odd Couple* (1965), and *The Apple Tree* (1966). These successes brought him a bid to put Elizabeth Taylor through her paces in the movie version *Who's Afraid of Virginia Woolf*. The paces were good enough to bring Liz an Oscar.

The following year, Nichols copped his own Oscar for *The Graduate* (1967). In outline, *The Graduate* does not sound much like Academy Award material, but Nichols carried along cast and story so adroitly that it all becomes engrossing and thoroughly believable.

In the story, Ben Braddock (Dustin Hoffman), on his return from college, is sexually pursued by Mrs. Robinson (Anne Bancroft), who has both a husband, and a daughter about Ben's age. Ben's family is worried by his listlessness and his refusal to find work. This situation continues through the summer. Ben's family decides he needs a girl to bring him out of the doldrums.Elaine (Katharine Ross), the daughter of Mrs. Robinson, with whom Ben has been spending nights in a hotel, is the choice.

Richard Burton and Elizabeth Taylor, a team of lovers well known in those days, starred in Nichols' *Who's Afraid of Virginia Woolf?* Copyright 1966 by Warner Brothers Productions.

Dustin Hoffman and Katharine Ross were the lovers who got together despite her mama's competition in *The Graduate*. Copyright 1967 by Embassy Pictures Corporation.

He agrees to date her, but hates it. He takes her to a strip tease place. Later he realizes how poorly he treated Elaine, and they begin dating regularly. Mrs. Robinson is outraged at her boy friend's attentions to her daughter. Bob, in turn, shocks Elaine by telling her the truth about himself and her mother. She goes back to Berkeley to college where her parents encourage her to marry Carl (Brian Avery) whom she was dating before she met Ben.

Ben learns of the projected wedding, but Mrs. Robinson tries to keep him from learning when and where it will be. He finally finds out, and, in the manner of Harold Lloyd in an earlier day, rushes to the church to stop the marriage. He interrupts as the final vows are being said. Elaine realizes then that she cannot marry Carl. Her parents try to stop her, but she breaks away and runs to Ben. They get out the door and lock everyone else inside by jamming a crucifix in the door handles. Then they grab a conveniently placed bus and ride away—presumably to happiness ever after.

The Graduate (1967), produced by Lawrence Thurman, Inc., for Embassy Pictures Corporation release. Directed by Mike Nichols. Screenplay by Calder Willingham and Buck Henry, from the novel by Charles Webb. Photographed by Robert Surtees. Principal cast members: Dustin Hoffman, Anne Bancroft, Katharine Ross.

Sir Carol Reed ponders a problem while filming *The Public Eye* (1972). Reed won his director's Oscar for *Oliver!* in 1968. Copyright 1972 by Universal Pictures Corporation.

1968

Carol Reed for Oliver!

Over the years, the kings and queens of England have seen fit to include a number of actors and actresses in their annual lists of honors, but directors have been less conspicuous when the knighthoods were passed out. Sir Carol Reed (b. 1906) was the first so honored, but, even then, he was not cited as a director. He was knighted for his contributions to motion pictures in Britain.

Great Britain has produced better and more popular directors than Carol Reed. However, he stayed at home and helped raise the quality of British-made films at a time when this quality was low indeed. No one begrudged him his knighthood. It was deserved.

Reed was born in London. He became an actor, but when this got him no place, he became a stage manager for Edgar Wallace. Wallace was then one of the most popular mystery writers in the world and also turned out a large number of plays. These he produced himself. Reed played parts in some of the plays and directed all the touring companies who took the plays to the provinces after their London run.

In 1930, Merian C. Cooper of RKO asked Wallace to come to Hollywood to polish the script for *King Kong*, the classic monster film. Before leaving, Wallace told Reed that talking pictures would soon take over from the stage. He advised the young man to study the new talking films intently. Reed took his advice, which came in handy when Wallace died in Hollywood. Reed did not have the experience to find an ordinary job in films, but sound saved him. He got a job as dialogue director in one of the British studios. Here, he learned enough about films to become a director.

Reed was fortunate to come along at a time when there was a government drive to increase the quality of British films. In 1927, a law was passed requiring one British film to be made for each film imported. This led to "quota production," turning out low budget films so that higher quality Hollywood products could be brought in. This law was changed in 1938 to encourage better quality home products.

Reed, who had been directing since 1935 when he made *Midshipman Easy*, met the new challenge with *The Stars Look Down* (1939). This was A.J. Cronin's story of a strike in the Welsh mining district. It was an unqualified success. Reed followed it with *Night Train* (1940) and a series of lesser vehicles during the war.

Reed is a slow, careful worker. He does not write his own scripts, but works closely with his writers during the development of the screenplay. From 1945, when he made a war documentary called *The True Glory*, with Garson Kanin as codirector, through 1960, when he made *Our Man in Havana*, Reed made only nine pictures. The best remembered of these is *The Third Man*, a masterpiece of moody suspense with Orson Welles and Joseph Cotton involved in Viennese intrigue. "*The Third Man Theme*," played on a zither, became as famous in its time as the "Colonel Bogey March" from the *River Kwai* did in a later time.

Reed then did two other films, *The Running Man* (1963) and *The Agony and the Ecstasy* (1968), with Charlton Heston impersonating the great genius Michaelangelo. Next, Carol Reed, whose best films had been suspense thrillers, shifted his style completely. He won his director's Oscar for a musical using the unlikely subject of Charles Dickens' *Oliver Twist*.

Oliver! was based upon the highly successful stage production by Lionel Bart. The story is so familiar it seems unnecessary to summarize it. However, it tells the tale of a young orphan, Oliver Twist (Mark Lester) who dares to ask the manager (Harry Secombe) of the orphanage for more food. The shocked manager sells the rebel into an apprenticeship. He runs away and is taken in by Fagin (Ron Moody), an old criminal who teaches boys to steal. Here there is a novel departure from the book. Dickens made Fagin a vicious criminal. The musical pictures him practically as a philanthropist who teaches boys to pickpocket to support

Joseph Cotten was the pursuer in Carol Reed's 1949 hit, *The Third Man,* based upon Graham Greene's thriller. Copyright 1949 by Selznick Releasing Corporation.

Charlton Heston was Michaelangelo in Sir Carol Reed's *The Agony and the Ecstasy.* Copyright 1965 by Twentieth Century-Fox Film Corporation.

Mark Lester wants more food in *Oliver!* This was a musical version of Charles Dickens' *Oliver Twist.* Copyright 1968 by Columbia Pictures Corporation.

themselves. Oliver is caught, but released to the care of Mr. Brownlow (Joseph O'Conor), a kindly man who later proves to be a relative. Oliver is then threatened by villainous Bill Sikes (Oliver Reed) who thinks Oliver will lead the police to him. But the would-be murderer is confounded, Oliver finds happiness, and Fagin—instead of being hanged as Dickens would have it—escapes to help other boys learn the pickpocketing trade.

Since Ron Moody plays Fagin as an engaging old rascal, we do not mind this perversion of a famous novel. It was good fun all the way, with Reed integrating music and story quite artfully for one working in a new genre.

Oliver! (1968), produced by John Woolf for Columbia Pictures Corporation release. Directed by Carol Reed. Screenplay by Vernon Harris, from Lionel Bart's stage production. Photographed by Oswald Morris. Principal cast members: Ron Moody, Mark Lester, Jack Wild, Harry Secombe, Oliver Reed, Joseph O'Conor.

John Schlesinger confers with his script writer, Waldo Salt, on *The Day of the Locust* set. Copyright 1975 by Long Road Productions.

1969

John Schlesinger for Midnight Cowboy

John Schlesinger (b. 1926) is a product of British documentary TV. He first got into theatricals through the University Players as an undergraduate at Oxford University. This led him first into acting and then to the British Broadcasting Company where he made short documentary films for the "Tonight" and "Monitor" shows.

Then he made a highly acclaimed forty-five-minute documentary about twenty-four hours in London's Waterloo Station, a film that received an award at the 1961 Venice Film Festival. The film dealt with the human comedy of people in a hurry to catch their trains. They ranged from a lost boy to a wedding party. Schlesinger described the film as showing under one roof a microcosm of the happiness, loneliness, rush, and misery of an entire world. This meant, presumably, that it was a cross-section of life.

It was remarkably well done, but, like so many documentaries, it was not true to life, although taken from life. By compressing a number of interesting events into forty-five minutes, the film gives the impression of a place where something intensely exciting is going on every moment. Actually, if one went to that place, he would possibly see one or two such things in the course of an entire day. It is much the same false premise as a biographical movie compressing 70 years of a famous person's life into 140 minutes.

Success in these documentaries led Schlesinger to his first feature film in 1962. This was *A Kind of Loving*, a story of a young man and woman who marry because she becomes pregnant. There is no real love, and the difference between them makes communications difficult. In the end, he decides to hang on and make the best of a bad bargain.

Schlesinger followed this film with *Billy Liar* (1963) and *Far From the Madding Crowd* (1967). Then, two years later, he made *Midnight Cowboy* (1969), the film that brought him the director's Oscar. The film also took top picture honors as well.

The story of *Midnight Cowboy* is a dirty, down-beat account of two genuine losers who cling to each other because they have nothing else. The screenplay by

Waldo Salt closely follows the book by James Leo Herlihy, but compresses the first part about the protagonist's life in Texas. This was necessary to fit into a normal running time.

It is the story of Joe Bush (Jon Voight), a dishwasher in a small Texas town. Sick of the place and his drab existence, Joe buys himself a fringed frontier jacket, a cowboy hat and boots, and sets out for New York by bus. He rather fancies his sexual prowess, believing he can make a living selling himself as a stud for lonely women.

During the bus ride, there are flashbacks to show his life in Texas. We are shown his abandoned mother and his swinging grandmother, along with the gang rape of Joe and his girlfriend (Jennifer Salt).

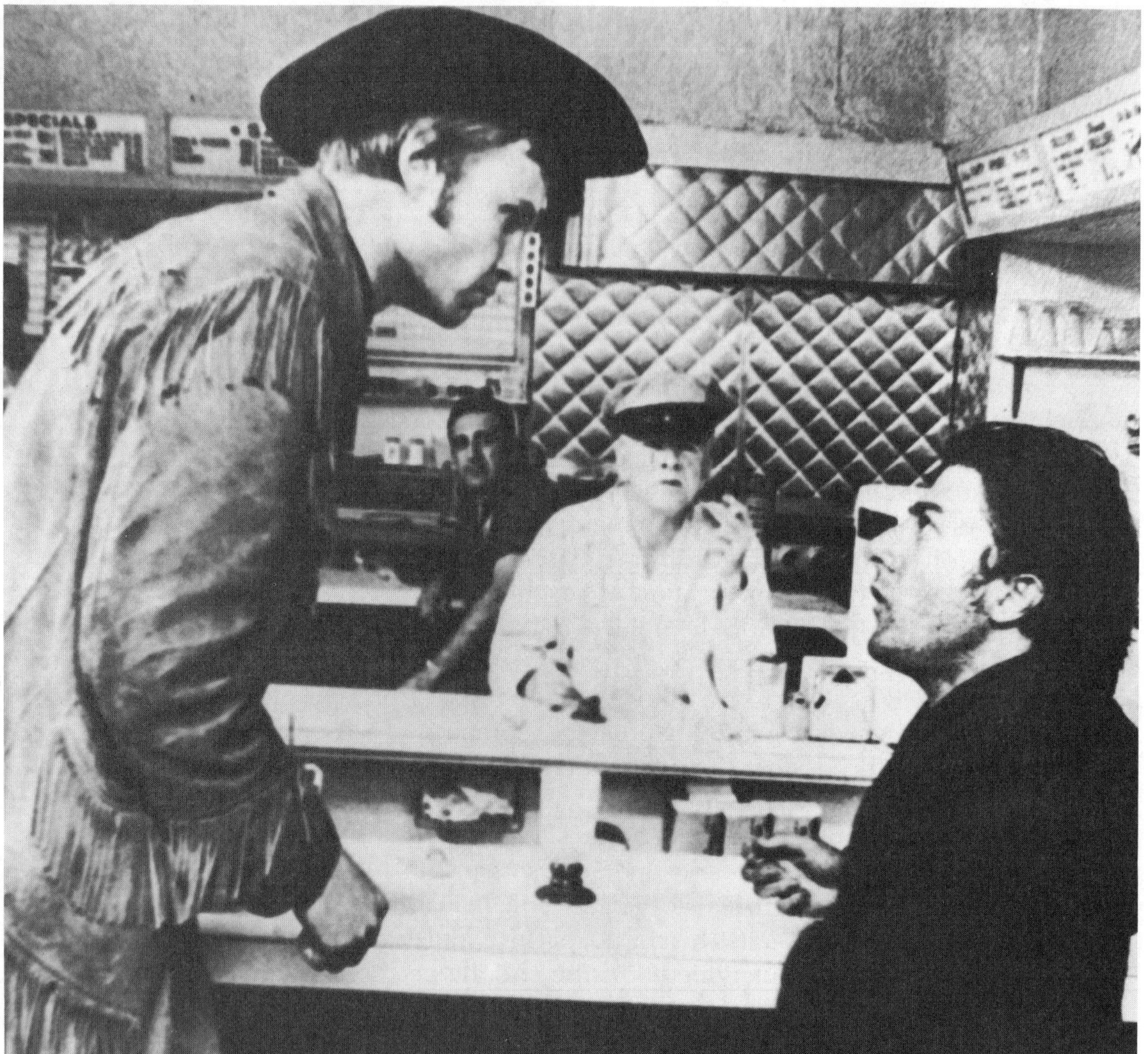

Jon Voight and Dustin Hoffman were a pair of losers drawn together by loneliness in *Midnight Cowboy*. Copyright 1967 by United Artists Corporation.

Jon Voight and Sarah Miles are a disappointment to each other in *Midnight Cowboy*. Copyright 1967 by United Artists Corporation.

Arriving in New York, Joe finds a room in a cheap hotel and picks up an aging blonde (Sylvia Miles). He not only gets no fee, but is stuck with a twenty-dollar taxi-fare. This is a clear indication that he will be as much a loser in New York as he was in Texas.

Joe then meets Ratso Rizzo (Dustin Hoffman), a crippled loser who suffers from tuberculosis. He offers to be Joe's pimp and find him both men and women. The first customer Ratso sends Joe is a religious fanatic. This causes a quarrel between Joe and Ratso, but they settle it because they are two lonely people who need each other. Joe moves into Ratso's dismal room in a rattrap building.

Although *Midnight Cowboy* was an X-rated film, the relationship between the two men is not homosexual. It is mutual loneliness. Ratso talks of his dream of going to Florida to live at Miami Beach. Business is poor for Joe. The young boy he picks up in a theater balcony turns out to have no money to pay. And so it goes until winter comes. This puts Ratso in bed. Joe, to get money to take his friend to Florida, brutally beats an aging homosexual and steals his money.

Joe and Ratso take off for Florida and their dream of an easy life in the sun. Ratso dies as they reach Miami. The film ends with Joe clinging to the dead body of the only real friend he ever had.

This is pretty grim fare for a popular film, but Schlesinger managed to bring out sympathy for the two unfortunates that captured the audience's feelings. Instead of disgust, one felt sorry for them. Schlesinger's documentary background provided a definite air of realism, heightened by filming on location in Texas, New York, and Florida. There was also a curious religious air that ran through the film. On the way to New York, there is a flash of a sign saying "Jesus Saves." Then the religious fanatic homosexual wants Joe to pray with him, and a picture of Christ hangs over the bed in the miserable room he shares with Ratso. It is not exactly clear what this all means. Perhaps the director was trying to say in a clumsy way that religion has failed those who need it most.

One thing is certain, however. Schlesinger very ably caught the lonesome spirit of a big city, fully earning his Academy Award. From this, one would have thought that he would have done an equally superb job showing the seamy side of Hollywood in *The Day of the Locust* (1975), but this picturization of Nathanael West's famous novel was as big a failure as *Midnight Cowboy* was a success.

Midnight Cowboy (1969), produced by Jerome Hellman for United Artists Corporation release. Directed by John Schlesinger. Screenplay by Waldo Salt, from the novel by James Leo Herlihy. Photographed by Alan Holander. Principal cast members: Dustin Hoffman, Jon Voight, Brenda Vaccaro, Sylvia Miles, John McGiver, Ruth White.

Paul Jabara (in drag) cuddles Donald Sutherland to the amusement of Karen Black and William Atherton in *The Day of the Locust*. Copyright 1975 by Long Road Productions.

Franklin J. Schaffner's films cover a wide range of subjects, from *The Planet of the Apes* to *Patton*.

1970

Franklin J. Schaffner for Patton

The Planet of the Apes, that far-out science fiction thriller, and *Patton* are about as far apart in style, content, and appeal as one can find in any director's credits. Yet both are the directorial creations of Franklin J. Schaffner (b. 1920).

Schaffner is a quiet, rather withdrawn man, as befits his missionary background. He was born in Tokyo, Japan. After his missionary father's death, the boy returned to Pennsylvania to grow up. World War II came along, and Schaffner spent two and a half years in the U.S. Navy.

He had intended to be a lawyer, but returned from the service with no more interest in a legal career. Some contacts got him a job on *The March of Time*, the news documentary sponsored by Time-Life. From here Schaffner moved on to the Columbia Broadcasting System just as television was getting started with live drama. Before long, Schaffner had graduated to directing for *Playhouse 90*, one of the top dramatic anthologies of the period.

Schaffner made his mark before live drama gave way to filmed material on TV, winning four Emmys, the TV equivalent of the Oscar, for his work.

As situation comedies crowded out drama on the electronic screen, Schaffner moved to Hollywood to direct Joanne Woodward in *The Stripper*. This was followed by *The Best Man* (1964), and then Charlton Heston in the epic *The War Lord* in 1965. Then, for 1967, he made *The Double Man* and the surprisingly successful *The Planet of the Apes*. Based upon Pierre Boulle's novel, this science fiction film featured Charlton Heston caught on a planet where intelligent apes were the dominant species. Then came *Patton*, which had its initial showing in New York on 30 December 1969, with general release following in February 1970.

Patton had been a long-time dream of producer Frank McCarthy, but no backer could be found with faith in a biography of a war glorifier. This was a time of American involvement in Vietnam and strong national anti-war fever. However, Darryl F. Zanuck's *The Longest Day* proved that the public would buy war epics. Still, no one wanted to take a chance on *Patton* until McCarthy went where he should have gone first: to Zanuck.

The project was well under way before Franklin J. Schaffner was brought in as director. George C. Scott had already been selected for the Patton role, and

Francis Ford Coppola—later to direct *The Godfather*—was writing the script. Coppola left to take on a directing job, and Edmund North finished the script.

George C. Scott is not the easiest person in the world to direct, and there were rumors of conflict on the set. These seem to have been somewhat exaggerated. Schaffner is a reserved man. He does not fraternize with the cast after hours on locations. McCarthy said Schaffner ate alone and spent his evening studying the script for the next day's shooting. Scott, as usual, tried to rewrite the script, and, when he couldn't get his way, sometimes took off on an all-day drunk. Schaffner shot around him and said nothing.

While making some concession to dramatic requirements, *Patton* was a remarkably accurate film biography. It ably caught the color and pity of a prince of war mongers. He was known as "Blood and Guts" Patton, and his men came up with a wry twist, "Yeah, *our* blood and *his* guts."

After a spectacular opening shot of the flamboyant Patton in front of a huge American flag, the plotless story begins with Patton recouping American fortunes after the disastrous defeat by Field Marshal Rommel's tank corps at Kasserine Pass in North Africa. Revitalized by Patton's dramatic leadership, the American tank forces plunge on to drive the Germans out of North Africa.

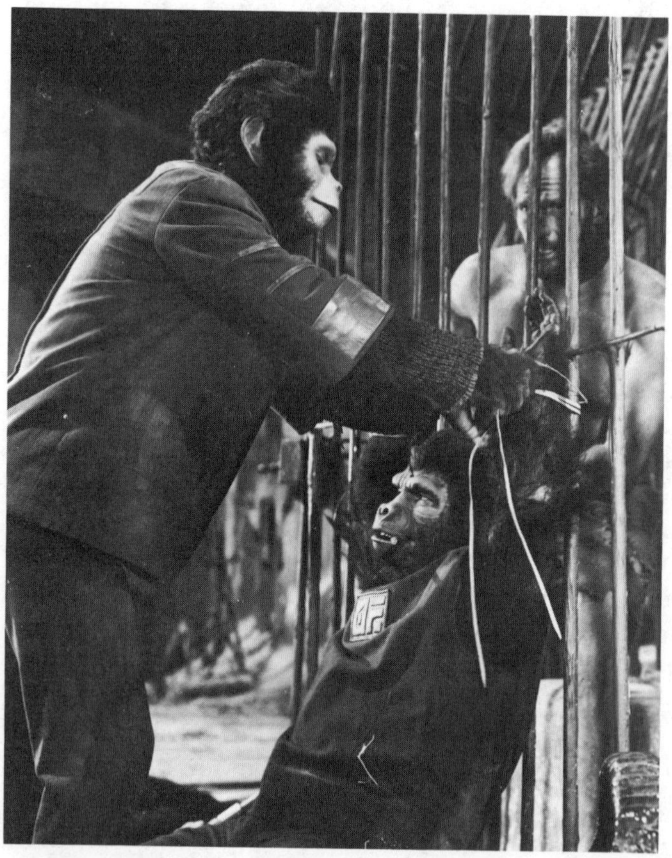

Charlton Heston and ape jailer in the unusual success *The Planet of the Apes*. Copyright 1967 by Twentieth Century-Fox Film Corporation.

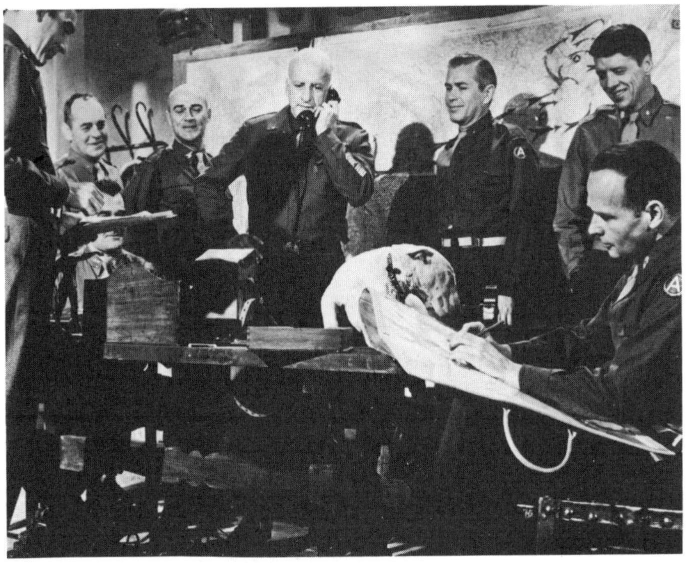

George C. Scott, center, gave a marvelous impersonation of *Patton*. Copyright 1970 by Twentieth Century-Fox Film Corporation.

Papillon (1973) with Steve McQueen was one of Schaffner's lesser efforts.

Patton then expects to lead the attack across the Mediterranean Sea against Palermo, Sicily. Instead he is assigned to protect the flank of Field Marshal Montgomery's British army, who will lead the attack. Montgomery and Patton are both hungry for glory. Patton, without orders, pushes ahead and captures Messina, the chief seaport of Sicily, thereby stealing Montgomery's thunder. This is followed by the notorious incident where Patton slaps a shell-shocked soldier and is removed from command by General Eisenhower.

Restored to command later, Patton dramatically rescues a trapped airborne force in the Battle of the Bulge. He then makes a lightning thrust deep into Czechoslovakia before politics forces him to halt so that Montgomery and the Russians can finish the fighting. Then, with no place in a peacetime army, he is removed from command.

Scott gave a gripping performance as the glory-mad general who was convinced that he had, through reincarnation, fought in every great war since the fall of Troy. Scott's performance was supported admirably by carefully planned battle scenes that were accurate. And well they should have been, for General Omar Bradley himself was technical advisor for the film. In the real war, Bradley had first been Patton's subordinate and then his boss.

None of Schaffner's subsequent films, including *Papillon* (1973), has approached the quality of *Patton*.

Patton (1970), produced by Frank McCarthy-Franklin J. Schaffner for Twentieth Century-Fox Film Corporation release. Directed by Franklin J. Schaffner. Screenplay by Francis Ford Coppola and Edmund H. North. Principal cast members: George C. Scott, Karl Malden.

William Friedkin's documentary approach worked well for the true-life *The French Connection.* Here the director is shown on the set of *The Exorcist,* which he filmed in 1973. Copyright 1973 by Warner Brothers Incorporated.

1971

William Friedkin for The French Connection

In reviewing *The French Connection*, the New York *Times*—a paper not given to extolling those who make cops and robbers films—had this to say: ". . . William Friedkin, a director whose previous work (*The Birthday Party* and *The Night They Raided Minsky's*) may not have prepared anyone for the excellence of this one."

Then, on the opposite side of the United States, the academy voter also took a favorable view of Mr. Friedkin and his picture, and even threw in a best actor Oscar for Gene Hackman, the star. This is even more surprising when we consider that the film colony as a group has never—at least not in real life—much liked police brutality and busting their second best source of amusement, dope pushers. And that is what *The French Connection* is about.

William Friedkin (b. 1930) was born in Chicago and started out as a mailroom boy at WGN-TV. Within two years, he had wrangled his way into directing live shows. Later, he shifted to WBKB-TV, where he got his first experience with film. He made the documentary *The People vs. Paul Krump*, a sixteen-millimeter film about a man who spent eleven years in death row. The station, while admitting its excellence, decided against broadcasting the film. Friedkin, on the basis of the film's superiority, was put in charge of the station's documentary unit.

The film was eventually shown at the 1962 San Francisco Film Festival, where it won the Golden Gate Award. This brought Friedkin to the attention of producer David Wolper. Wolper hired Friedkin to make three television documentaries for ABC-TV. They were *The Thin Blue Line*, about law enforcement; *Mayhem on a Sunday Afternoon*, about professional football; and *The Bold Men*, about those who risk their lives for science, adventure, or money.

Friedkin's first feature film was *Good Times* (1967), which was also the screen debut of Sonny and Cher. This was good enough to get him the directorial assignment on *The Night They Raided Minsky's* (1968). He made two other films, *The Birthday Party* (1968), and *The Boys in the Band* (1970), before hitting big with *The French Connection* in 1971.

In many ways, *The French Connection* is a throwback to the gangster movies of the early thirties. There are shooting, suspense, a wild chase, and the villains get it in the last reel. The chase and the shoot-outs are in the grand tradition. The only concession to the times is that the cops are not white-hat boys. We see this early in the film when Jim Doyle (Gene Hackman) pistol whips a black drug-pusher.

The film exactly fitted Friedkin's documentary style, for it was based upon the true story of two New York detectives, Eddie Eagan and Sonny Grosso, who broke a $32 million heroin-smuggling scheme in 1962. The names were changed to Jimmy Doyle and Buddy Russo for the film.

The story deals with the attempt of a New York pusher's "French connection" to smuggle the heroin into the United States by hiding it in a Lincoln Continental belonging to a French TV-personality.

Part of the fascination lies in the way we are shown how the scheme works. So, despite some fictionalizing (the elevated train chase, for example, did not occur in the real case), we are seeing the real thing. *The French Connection* is fact-fiction at its best.

We are able to follow the entire smuggling operation from its initial deal in Marseilles, France, to the final bust on Ward's Island in New York. The climax is a suspenseful chase between a car and a hijacked elevated train.

The film was criticized for failure to characterize any of the cast except Hackman. But for the public—and apparently for the academy voters as well—all faults were forgotten in the excitement of the chase.

Friedkin followed this success with another, *The Exorcist* (1973), but it failed to impress the academy voters.

Friedkin's second film was *The Night They Raided Minsky's* (1978).

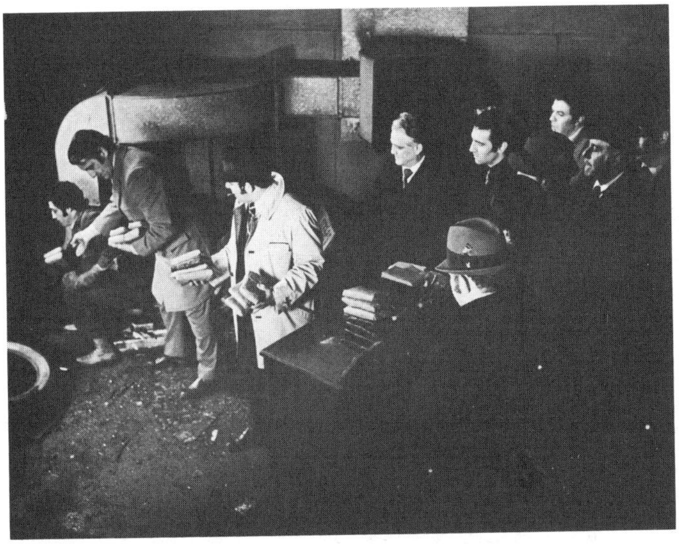

Here it is—$32 million in pure heroin—the prize for the long chase that made up *The French Connection.* Copyright 1971 by Twentieth Century-Fox Film Corporation.

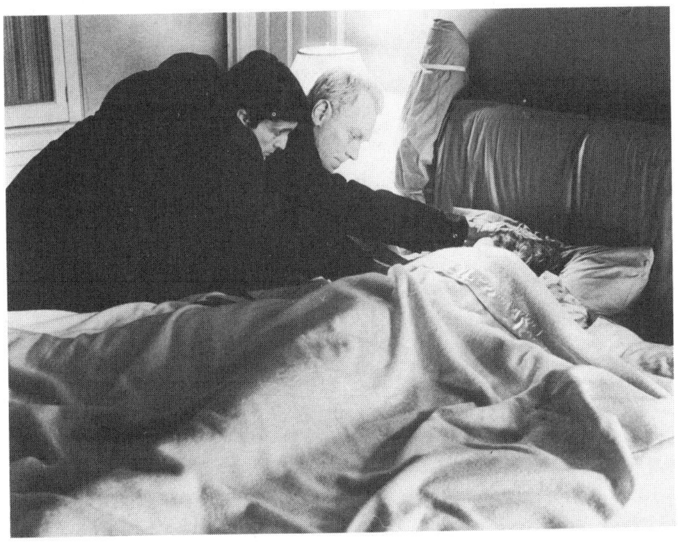

The Exorcist (1973), a weird tale of demonic possession, was Friedkin's next film after *The French Connection.* Copyright 1973 by Warner Brothers Incorporated.

The French Connection (1971), produced by Phillip Antoni for Twentieth Century-Fox Film Corporation release. Directed by William Friedkin. Screenplay by Ernest Tidyman, from the nonfiction book by Robin Moore. Photographed by Owen Roizman. Principal cast members: Gene Hackman, Fernando Rey, Roy Schneider, Tony LaBlanco, Marcel Bozzuffi.

Fosse came to Hollywood with a string of Broadway hits behind him. Copyright 1972 by Allied Artists-ABC Pictures.

1972

Bob Fosse for Cabaret

Bob Fosse (b. 1927) came to Hollywood touted as the logical successor to Fred Astaire. He had made quite a name for himself as a dancer in Broadway productions. But, when he arrived in 1953, musicals took one of their periodic drops. After appearing in *Give a Girl a Break*, *My Sister Eileen*, and a couple of others, Fosse headed back to the more congenial atmosphere of New York.

But in 1968 he was back again. This time, there were plenty to agree that he might well be the successor to Astaire, at least as a choreographer. Since he had left Hollywood the first time, Fosse had collected five Tony awards for his Broadway endeavors, the first for the choreography of *Pajama Game* in 1955. Such hits as *Damn Yankees*, *New Girl in Town*, *Redhead*, and *Sweet Charity* followed. Fosse choreographed them all and was also director for *Redhead* and *Sweet Charity*. He was choreographer on the big hits *Little Me* and *How to Succeed in Business without Really Trying*. He also did the screen choreography for the film versions of *Pajama Game* and *Damn Yankees*.

So, when he came back in 1968 to direct *Sweet Charity* for the screen, Fosse had reached the top. The long climb started in Chicago when he was born into a theatrical family. He made his first professional appearance as a dancer when he was thirteen. After time out to serve with the U.S. Navy in World War II, he landed a spot in the touring company of *Call Me Mister*. Then, after two Broadway shows, Hollywood beckoned the first time.

After directing *Sweet Charity*, with Shirley MacLaine taking the Broadway role done by Fosse's wife Gwen Verdon, Fosse waited four years before directing another film. It was worth waiting for. The film was *Cabaret*, a penetrating look at the decadent life of 1929 Berlin. The setting, the time, and the decadence invite comparison with Josef von Sternberg's *The Blue Angel* (1929). In making the comparison, we should say that Liza Minnelli is not a Marlene Dietrich, nor is Marlene a Liza. Each in her own way was incomparable in the similar role of a cheap night-club floozie.

In the major awards, *Cabaret* lost to *The Godfather*, but Fosse got the director's award, Minnelli took the best actress, and Joel Grey was best supporting actor.

Cabaret was a brilliant job for coordinating music and story. It opens with Joel Grey in strange white makeup singing "Willkomen" to patrons of the Kit Kat Club. Then we pick up British language student Brian Roberts (Michael York), who rents a room next door to Sally Bowles (Liza Minnelli), a singer at the Kit Kat. Hardly top drawer in morals and ability, Sally hopes the club will afford her a stepping stone into films. The two become romantically involved as the growing Nazi menace begins to pollute Berlin. We are shown what is happening when hoodlums beat the manager of the Kit Kat club for having two boisterous Nazis thrown out. This goes on while Grey is singing a bouncy musical number.

The lives of Sally and Brian become entwined with the Jewish daughter of a department store owner (Marisa Berensen) and a German youth (Fritz Wepper). The romance between the two is complicated by her religion.

Sally becomes involved with the wealthy Max (Helmut Griem). She admits this to Brian. He storms out and is beaten by Nazi hoodlums. Then, when Sally becomes pregnant, Brian tells her that he will still take care of the child. She refuses, choosing an abortion. At this point, Brian gives up on her. They embrace for the last time. Then Sally goes to the Kit Kat to sing her song: "Life is a cabaret . . ."

Fosse also directed the less popular but fine *Lenny* (1975).

On his first trip to Hollywood, Bob Fosse was a dancer in *My Sister, Eileen* with Janet Leigh. Copyright 1954 by Columbia Pictures Corporation.

Dustin Hoffman was *Lenny* in Fosse's 1975 picture of that name. Copyright 1975 by United Artists Corporation.

Cabaret, with Joel Gray (center) and Liza Minnelli (half-hidden at right), earned Fosse the director's Oscar for 1972. Copyright 1972 by Allied Artists-ABC Pictures.

Cabaret (1972), produced by Cy Feuer for Allied Artists-ABC Pictures release. Directed by Bob Fosse. Screenplay by Jay Allen. Photographed by Geoffrey Unsworth. Principal cast members: Liza Minnelli, Joel Grey, Michael York, Helmut Griem, Marisa Berensen.

George Roy Hill with Robert Crawford (left) was a well-known Broadway director before coming to Hollywood. Copyright 1974 by Universal City Studios.

1973

George Roy Hill for The Sting

George Roy Hill (b. 1922) set out to be a musician, but ended up as actor, director, and aviator. After studying music at Yale and Trinity College, Dublin, Ireland, Hill became an actor. Then World War II took him into aviation, and the Korean conflict continued his flying career.

After this, he turned his back on the military, becoming an actor and writer, and then a TV director. This led him to Broadway, where he directed *The Gang's All Here, Greenwillow, Look Homeward, Angel,* and *Period of Adjustment.*

Period of Adjustment was bought for films, and Hill went along to direct the film version for a 1962 release. He stayed to make *Toys in the Attic* (1963), *The World of Henry Orient* (1964), James Michener's sprawling *Hawaii* (1966), *Thoroughly Modern Millie* (1967), and then, in 1969, the blockbuster *Butch Cassidy and the Sundance Kid* for which he received his first Academy Award nomination.

The symbolism and esoteric meanings so dear to the hearts of some reviewers are bypassed by Hill in favor of action and sharp characterization. His adroit interplay of characters requires a sure hand in casting. This means that the director must assert himself very strongly, for casting is usually the province of the producer.

Hill can show quite a bit of stubbornness—and patience, as well—in holding out for the stars he wants and sees as ideal for a part. In the case of *Butch Cassidy*, he was satisfied with Paul Newman in the role of Butch, but he was relieved when Marlon Brando turned down the Sundance Kid role. Brando was rather old for the role and also difficult to handle.

Hill then suggested Robert Redford. Zanuck wanted Warren Beatty and threatened to pull Hill off the picture if he kept insisting on Redford. Hill then called in reinforcements and kept battling. He got both Paul Newman and writer William Goldman to back him up on Redford.

This was not stubbornness. He saw Robert Redford as the best casting for the role, even though Beatty was certainly more famous than Redford at this point. Redford's only really good notices had come from *Barefoot in the Park,* and not too many were betting on his reaching the top of the ladder.

Redford justified all the faith Hill put in him. His part contributed to the extraordinary success of this comic and tragic western. But, more important, it established the team that Hill would use for *The Sting*, the 1973 Best Picture of the Year and Best Achievement in Direction.

Like *Butch Cassidy*, *The Sting* has bad-guy heroes. But those who feel uncomfortable when crooks win can ease their consciences while viewing *The Sting* because the crooked protagonists are Robin Hoodishly engaged in fleecing a bigger crook.

Thoroughly Modern Millie, with Julie Andrews and James Fox, was Hill's fourth Hollywood film. Copyright 1967 by Universal Pictures Corporation.

Robert Redford was also in Hill's 1975 story of barnstorming pilots, *The Great Waldo Pepper*.

Johnny Hooker (Redford) is a member of a small-time con gang. They mistakenly get $11,000 from a numbers runner, and the numbers chief, Lonnegan (Robert Shaw), wants revenge. He kills the leader of the con gang and starts looking for the rest. He does not know who Hooker is, but Hooker knows it is only a matter of time before Lonnegan's killers find him. Instead of running, he plots revenge for his friend's death.

This takes the form of a million-dollar con against Lonnegan. To do this, Hooker enlists the aid of Harry Gondorff (Newman), a really top con-man. Gondorff arranges for Lonnegan to "discover" that Gondorff has a secret means of getting race track results before the bookie joints do. This permits him to make sure-thing bets. Hooker pretends to doublecross Gondorff and lets Lonnegan in on a fix. At the same time, another doublecross is on. An FBI man threatens Hooker unless he betrays Gondorff, but Hooker gets him to hold off until after "the sting," when Lonnegan is conned out of his million.

Hooker tips off Lonnegan, who tells him he has bet a million, but then Hooker tells Lonnegan that he made the wrong bet. The numbers chief now realizes that Hooker and Gondorff were in cahoots to con him. He demands his money back. At this point, the FBI man bursts in. There is gunfire, and Hooker and Gondorff fall. Lonnegan takes advantage of the melee to flee. Then Hooker and Gondorff sit up laughing. The fake FBI man is all part of the con to make Lonnegan think they have been killed so he will not try to seek them out again. Gondorff takes the million. Hooker refuses his part. He feels well paid in getting revenge on Lonnegan and in learning from Gondorff how to swing a big con.

The similarity in cast and underworld background invites comparison between *Butch Cassidy* and *The Sting*, but actually there is little similarity. The relationship between the characters is different, as is the setting and treatment. In *Butch Cassidy*, the play is more for fun. *The Sting*, while not without humor, is played straight. The humor arises from the situations rather than wisecracks.

Also, *The Sting* is more suspenseful. It is more tightly written, with a steady buildup to the surprise ending. Our attention is caught all the way. The settings, unlike many so-called excursions into nostalgia, do not intrude. They convey the sense and feeling of the 1930s in a way that makes us absorb them, rather than feel they are rammed down our throats.

And, of course, Hill had two perfectly cast actors who meshed together wonderfully, as he knew they would when he first insisted on having Redford for *Butch Cassidy*.

The Sting (1973), produced by Tony Bill, Michael and Julia Phillips, for Zanuck-Brown-Universal Pictures Corporation release. Directed by George Roy Hill. Screenplay by David S. Ward. Photographed by Robert Surtees. Principal cast members: Paul Newman, Robert Redford, Robert Shaw, Ray Walston, Charles Durning.

Robert Redford runs from hit men in *The Sting*, the picture that won Hill his director's Oscar. Copyright 1973 by Universal Pictures Corporation.

Francis Ford Coppola, with daughter Sophia Carmina, contemplates a scene during the filming of *The Godfather II*. Copyright 1974 by Paramount Pictures Corporation and the Coppola Company.

1974

Francis Ford Coppola for The Godfather Part II

"Sequels are never equals," playwright George S. Kaufman once said. Generally, history will bear him out, but *The Godfather Part II* is a big exception. It took the top-picture Oscar despite losing the original *Godfather's* biggest star, Marlon Brando.

Oddly enough, the director, Francis Ford Coppola (b. 1939) did not want to make *The Godfather Part II*. He himself has said, "But Paramount made me an offer I could not refuse."

Coppola was born in Detroit, Michigan. His father was a conductor of musical comedies, and the boy was involved in the theater for as far back as he can remember. He loved films from the beginning. By 1948, when he was nine years old, he was using a home recorder to make sound tracks for the family's amateur movies. An attack of polio then put him in bed for a year. During this time, he further developed his sense of drama by working with puppets.

Eventually, he enrolled in the University of California at Los Angeles (UCLA). Here he was a part of an intense group of young film technique students who all thought they could remold the motion picture industry if given a chance. While at UCLA, Coppola won the $2000 Samuel Goldwyn Award for a script he wrote. This brought him sufficient recognition to get him hired by Roger Corman. At the beginning of the 1960s, Corman had five years of solid success as a maker of horror, and rock-and-roll movies.

His jobs with Corman included directing dialogue for *The Tower of London* (1962), with Boris Karloff, and handling sound for *The Young Racers* (1962). He kept pestering Corman to let him direct. So, this same year, the producer gave him a title, *Dementia*, and told Coppola to write a script around the title and film it. The result was *Dementia 13*.

It did nothing to start producers demanding his services as a director, but he developed quite a reputation as a writer. Among the scripts he worked on were *Is Paris Burning?* (1966), *This Property Is Condemned* (1966), and *Reflections in a Golden Eye* (1967).

In the meantime, he bought film rights to a novel called *You're a Big Boy Now,* wrote a script, and got a package together that included himself as director. It was released in 1967. He then got the directorial assignment for *Finian's Rainbow* (1968), with Fred Astaire and Petula Clark in a twenty-year-old musical comedy. It was not overly successful.

Later, Coppola became involved in the script for *Patton*, but withdrew when the opportunity to direct *The Godfather* came his way.

Coppola's reputation as a director did not warrant putting him on a picture of *The Godfather's* ultimate magnitude. However, Paramount originally conceived it as a programmer to try to cash in on the book's popularity. Several directors turned it down before it was offered to Coppola. He immediately saw tremendous possibilities, and his enthusiasm was great enough to convince Paramount to increase the budget and get Brando for the pivotal role of Don Corleone, the Mafia chief.

The result was an Academy Award for the best picture of 1972 and a best actor award for Brando. Coppola lost out in the director's Oscar race to Bob Fosse for *Cabaret*.

The enormous financial and critical success of *The Godfather* naturally suggested a sequel to Paramount. Coppola was reluctant, and Brando flatly refused to replay his role of Don Corleone. Brando stuck by his refusal, but Coppola gave in to a $1 million salary and the promise of a completely free hand in making the picture.

The result was not a sequel in the true sense. Coppola and Mario Puzo, the original author, worked out a combination of the stories of Don Corleone and his son which was more like a frame around the original picture, dealing with the years both before and after *The Godfather* film. Thus, the theme is the rise of Don

Barbara Hancock is a dancing partner for Fred Astaire in *Finian's Rainbow*. Copyright 1968 by Warner Bros.-Seven Arts Incorporated.

Marlon Brando won an Oscar for his role in Coppola's *The Godfather.* Copyright 1972 by Paramount Pictures Incorporated.

Lee Strasberg and Al Pacino were in Coppola's *The Godfather II.* Copyright 1974 by Paramount Pictures Corporation and the Coppola Company.

Corleone in the Mafia and the later decline of his son. Robert de Niro was the young Don Corleone and Al Pacino was Michael Corleone, the son.

The result was six Oscars, including best picture, direction, supporting actor, art direction, screenplay, and original score. This is three more than *The Godfather* got.

The Godfather Part II (1974), produced by Francis Ford Coppola for Paramount Pictures Corporation release. Directed by Francis Ford Coppola. Screenplay by Coppola and Mario Puzo, from sections of Puzo's novel. Photographed by Gordon Willis. Principal cast members: Al Pacino, Robert Duvall, Robert deNiro, Diane Keaton, Talia Shire, Lee Strasberg, and Michael V. Gazzo.

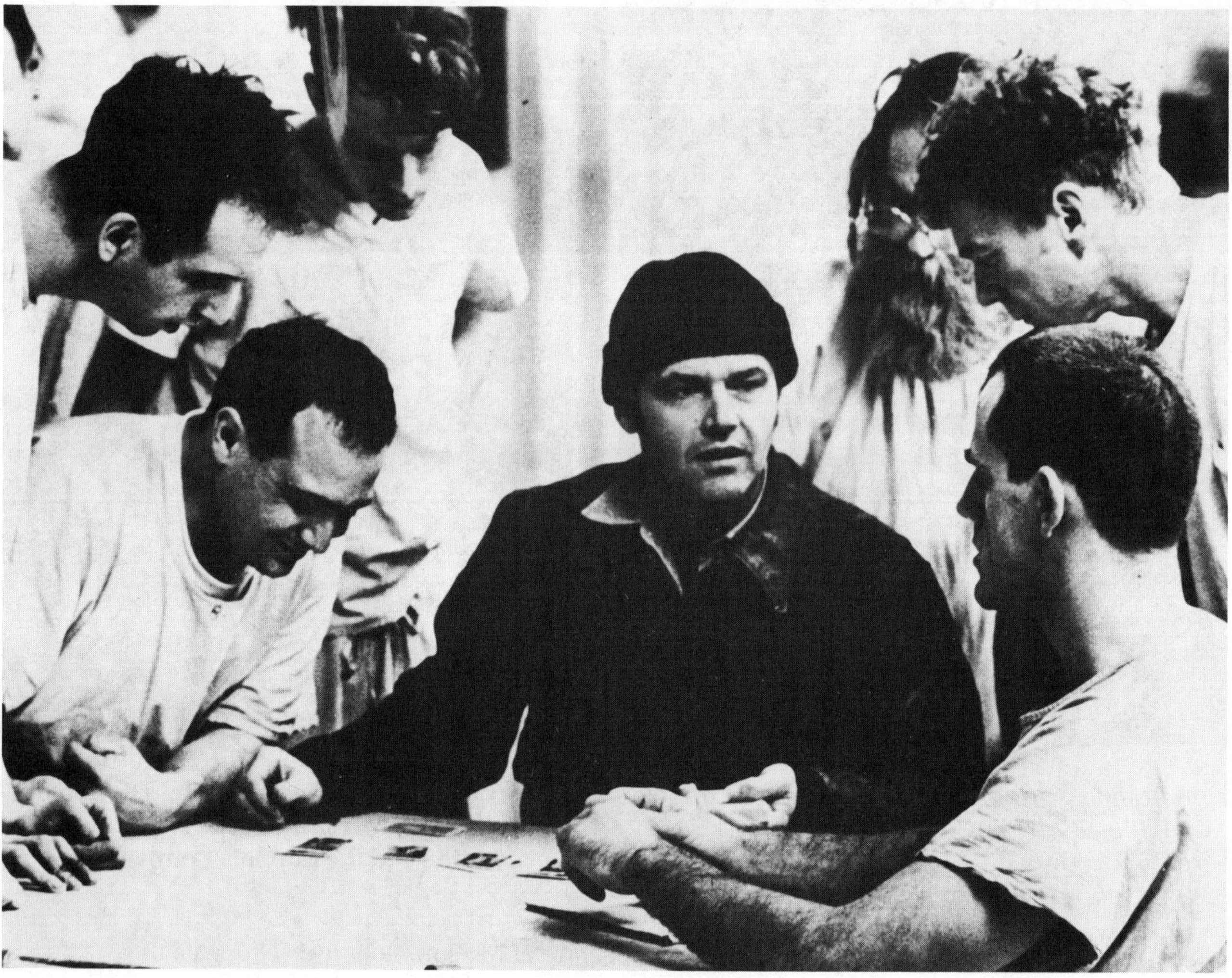

Jack Nicholson (center) with Danny Vito (left) and Christopher Lloyd (right) in *One Flew over the Cuckoo's Nest.* Despite some friction during filming, the picture made a grand sweep of the top four academy categories: best picture, best actor, best actress, and best director. Copyright 1975 by Fantasy Films and United Artists Corporation.

1975

Milos Forman for One Flew over the Cuckoo's Nest

They had to go to Czechoslovakia to find a director to show how crazy some Americans are, but that's Hollywood for you. As it turned out, the producers made a very good choice. Milos Forman (b. 1932) had established himself as a keen observer of the peculiarities of ordinary people, especially young ones. *One Flew over the Cuckoo's Nest* was definitely not about ordinary people, and the resulting picture is certainly a tribute to Forman's versatility.

Although set in a mental institution, *Cuckoo* was at the opposite end of the pole from horror films like *The Snake Pit*. It put a swaggering con-man in a confrontation with hospital authority. In his own individual way, McMurphy (Jack Nicholson) was an amoral, nastier version of TV's famous Sergeant Bilko. He was out to con everybody and frustrate discipline right to the breaking point. The result was a black comedy that drew laughs from human misfortune. In the end, the humor turned to tragedy.

Forman was born in Caslav, Czechoslovakia, and he studied at the Academy of Music and Drama in Prague. He then became a radio announcer and script writer. This led him into movie making. He was first an assistant director, and then became a director in 1963. He developed quite a reputation in his native country until the political situation erupted in 1968. He came to the United States in 1971 to make *Taking Off* for Universal release. It was about a family whose daughter "took off"—that is, ran away. It was much less than successful.

This gained him an immediate reputation as one of those foreign imports who was long on art and short on commercial appeal. He was offered scripts, but he considered them all second-rate. He turned them down rather than besmirch his reputation further. Then he was offered *One Flew Over the Cuckoo's Nest*, a script based upon Ken Kesey's best-seller thirteen years before. It had been knocking around Hollywood for years. A lot of people had been interested in it, but none had the courage to tackle the extremely difficult job of trying to wring laughter out of madness in a grim institution.

In the story, McMurphy (Jack Nicholson) is a loud-mouthed, hard-fisted jailbird who has been committed to a mental institution. He is as shrewd as he is crazy, and sets out to dominate the ward. His quixotic attack on authority brings him into direct conflict with Miss Ratshed, the "Big Nurse" (Louise Fletcher). It is a battle of titans.

McMurphy upsets the group therapy meetings, organizes a basketball team, nudges the inmates toward insubordination, and makes a bet with them that he can get the Big Nurse's goat. He even persuades the doctor to give them a pass so they can go fishing. When the boat owner refuses to take mental defectives, McMurphy steals the boat.

The inmates, except for McMurphy, are defeated people. They have lost all will power and cannot cope with the outside. We see nurses, doctors, and attendants working to keep them this way so they will remain docile. Under McMurphy's rebellious prodding, which earns him a series of painful shock treatments, they begin to assert themselves slightly. We can see that McMurphy is good therapy for them. This is especially brought out when he smuggles into the institution a whore for a thirty-year-old cringing male virgin (Brad Dourif) who stutters badly. After the orgy, his stutter is cured until the Big Nurse finds out. She angrily says she will tell his mother. His slight improvement is destroyed and he is the cringing, begging, stuttering, defeated person he was before.

This causes McMurphy to attack the nurse, attempting to strangle her. She has him sent for a lobotomy, in which a section of his brain is removed to cure his homicidal tendencies. The swaggering, gambling, rebellious personality is gone. He is reduced to a dull vegetable. This is too much for his half-Indian friend, the Chief (Will Sampson). Out of pity, he smothers McMurphy with a pillow. Then the Chief breaks out a window and becomes the one who flew out of the cuckoo's nest.

Taking Off (1971) was Milos Forman's first American-made film. It was not successful. Copyright 1971 by Universal Pictures Corporation.

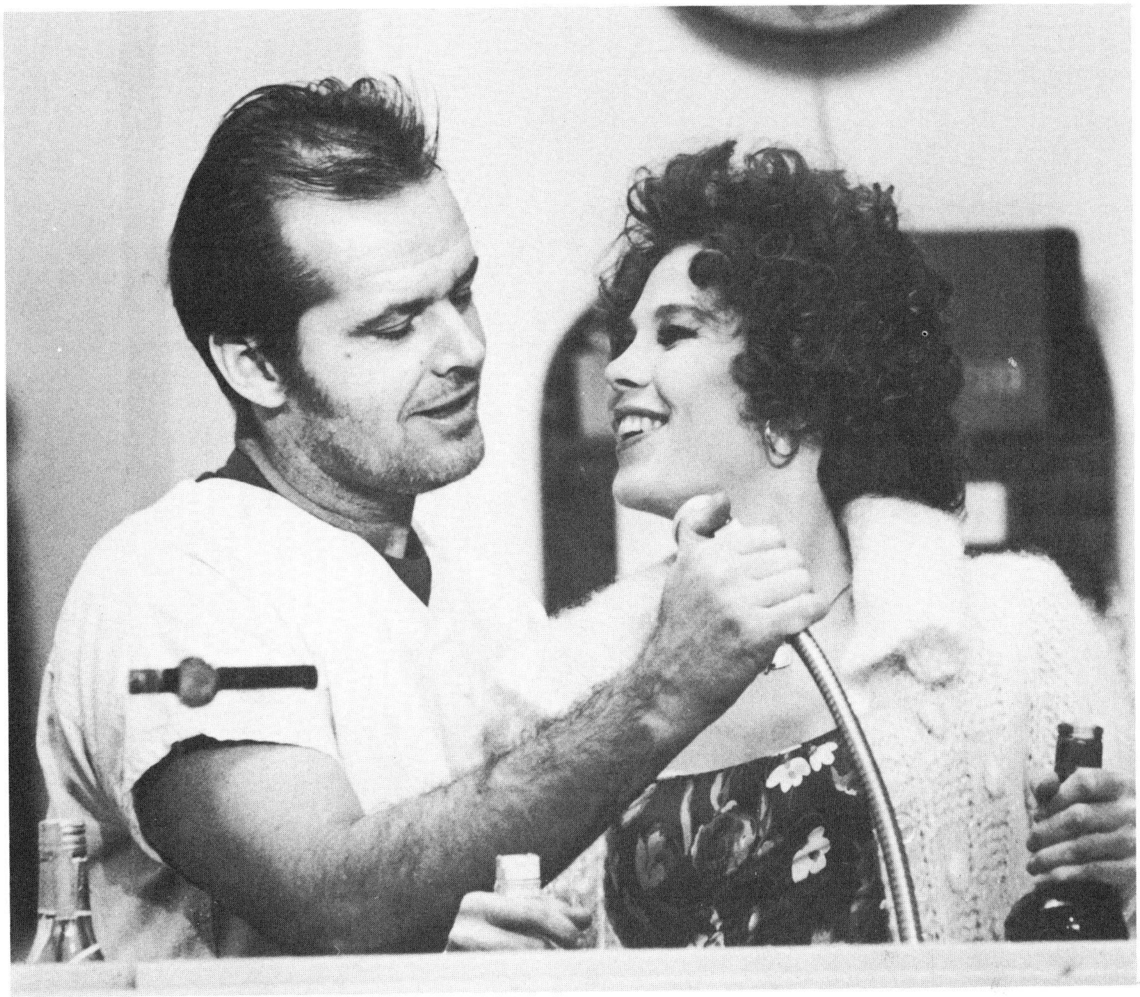

Jack Nicholson frolics with Marya Small in *One Flew over the Cuckoo's Nest.* Copyright 1975 by Fantasy Films and United Artists Corporation.

The film took awards for best picture, best actor (Nicholson), best actress (Louise Fletcher as the nurse), and best director. This is the first time since *It Happened One Night* in 1934 that any picture gained all four top spots. This is a genuine tribute to Forman as director. He would accept a name star (Nicholson) only in the McMurphy role. He insisted that unknowns, chosen for cast suitability, be in all the other roles.

One Flew Over the Cuckoo's Nest (1975), produced by Paul Zaentz and Michael Douglas for United Artists Corporation release. Directed by Milos Forman. Screenplay by Lawrence Hauben and Bo Goldman. Photographed by Haskell Wexler, William Fraker, Bill Butler. Principal cast members: Jack Nicholson, Louise Fletcher, Will Sampson, Brad Dourit, William Redfield, Peter Brocco, Marya Small.

John Avildsen took the 1976 director's Oscar for *Rocky*.
Copyright 1976 by United Artists Corporation.

1976

John Avildsen for Rocky

John Avildsen (b. 1935) was not a likely choice to make the triumphant march to the podium on Oscar night. It is true that he guided Jack Lemmon to a 1973 Oscar as best actor in *Save the Tiger*, but his track record as a director was not good.

Avildsen was born in Oak Park, Illinois, and got into the film business through advertising work. He began in commercial filming, working as a cameraman and anything else he could get to help him get started.

He helped on such pictures as the Otto Preminger picture *Hurry Sundown* (1965), and later directed *Joe*, *Cry Uncle*, *Save the Tiger*, and *W.W. and the Dixie Dancekings*.

During the casting of *W.W. and the Dixie Dancekings*, Avildsen auditioned a hungry young actor for a part. This was fate knocking on Avildsen's door, but he failed to recognize it. The young actor was Sylvester Stallone. Avildsen sent Sly on his way as not the type for the Dancekings role.

W.W. and the Dixie Dancekings, despite a good performance by Burt Reynolds in a con-man role that fitted him well, failed to set the world on fire. Neither did the succeeding Avildsen films. So no one was rushing to give him scripts to read. He stagnated and waited for the chance that was slow in coming. In the meantime, Stallone was not doing well, either. But he differed from the average young hopeful who waits for someone to give him a chance. He set out to make his own chance. He had seen *Easy Rider* and thought he could write a script that good. He says he bought a nineteen-cent ball point pen and a thirty-nine-cent pad of paper and began. While a lot of things and work came in between, the result, surprisingly enough, was the script for *Rocky*.

Other actors have tried to write themselves a script, but Stallone performed the near miracle of finding a couple of producers—Irwin Winkler and Robert Chartoff—who were willing to take it on. United Artists agreed to back it for $1 million and not a cent more. This is poverty-row financing in today's Hollywood.

It is usually the prerogative of the producers to pick the director, but Stallone was involved in every facet of this film. He helped choose John Avildsen. There was nothing in Avildsen's past to indicate he was a winner. But he had one asset in his favor: he would work cheap.

The natural question is how much of *Rocky* was Avildsen and how much was Stallone, who not only wrote the script, but did much of the casting, and even some of the direction?

Stallone paid high tribute to Avildsen. In his account of the filming of *Rocky*, Stallone tells of coming on a location set and finding Avildsen lying in a frozen gutter, lining up a shot with a viewfinder. Another time he told how Avildsen takes advantage of every opportunity and weaves in accidents into the filming. It would appear that Avildsen, despite Stallone's finger in all parts of the film pie, earned both his salary and his Oscar.

The story of *Rocky* is about a loser, Rocky Balboa (Sylvester Stallone), a plodding club-fighter who doubles as a collector for a loan shark by day. He meets Adrian (Talia Shire) who works in a pet shop and is as lonely as he. Her brother (Burt Young) is afraid Adrian is going to be an old maid and invites Rocky to Thanksgiving dinner hoping a romance will blossom. They hear a TV interview with arrogant Apollo Creed (Carl Weather), the heavyweight champion of the world.

Later, Creed's opponent in the upcoming championship match is injured. The other contenders refuse to fight on such short notice. Creed's promoters come up with a gimmick. They will offer a title shot to a local unknown as a symbol that anyone can rise to the top in America. The champ will carry the sucker for three rounds and then knock him out. From a list of possible fighters, they select "The Italian Stallion," Rocky Balboa.

Jack Lemmon had an Oscar-winning role of his own in John Avildsen's *Save the Tiger* (1973). Copyright 1972 by Paramount Pictures Corporation, Filmways Inc., Jalem Productions and Cirandinha Productions.

John Avildsen's *W.W. and the Dixie Dancekings* had Burt Reynolds (center) in the role of the con man. The dancekings, from left, are Jerry Reed, Don Williams, James Hampton, Conny Van Dyke, and Richard Hurst. Copyright 1975 by Twentieth Century-Fox Film Corporation.

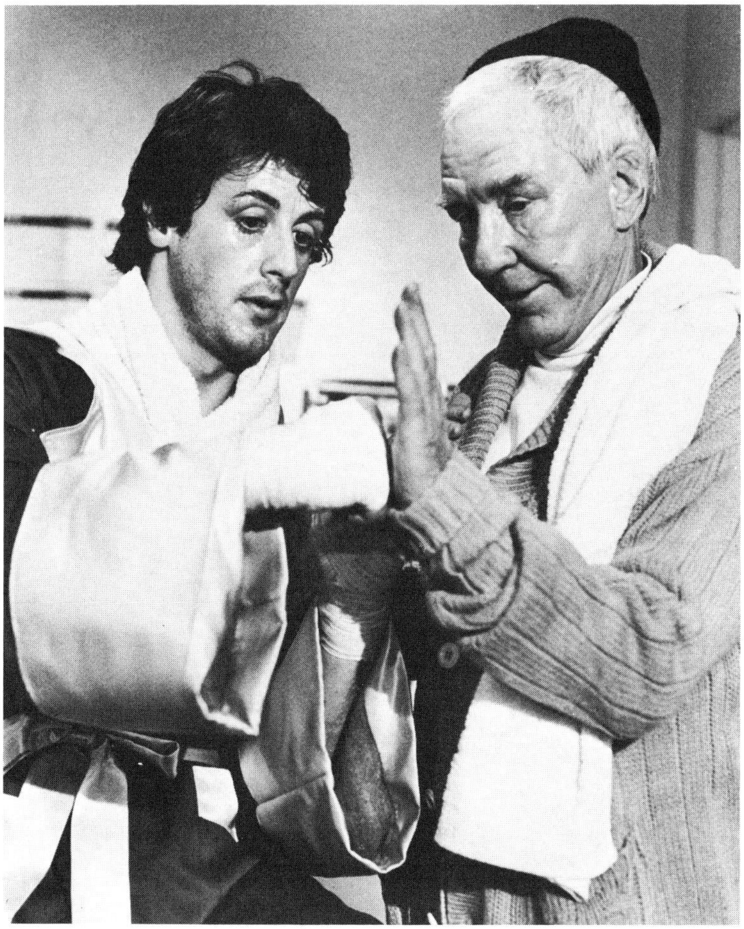

Sylvester Stallone was the fighter, and Burgess Meredith was his manager in *Rocky*. Copyright 1976 by United Artists Corporation.

He agrees to accept the challenge. In the meantime, he and Adrian draw closer together. He helps her overcome her shyness, and she gives him someone who cares at last. This causes him to throw himself into training as he never had before. He becomes a new man and gives the surprised champion the fight of his life. The fight—a technical marvel—was choreographed, and each action was rehearsed according to a written plan for both actors and camera movement. The result was a brutal exhibition, yet one of the most effective fight sequences ever put on film. The fight is a draw, permitting Creed to hold his championship, but it is also a victory for Rocky in that he proved himself at long last.

Rocky (1976), produced by Irwin Winkler and Robert Chartoff for United Artists Corporation release. Directed by John Avildsen. Screenplay and original story by Sylvester Stallone. Photographed by James Crabe. Principal cast members: Sylvester Stallone, Talia Shire, Burgess Meredith, Burt Young, Carl Weather, Joe Spinell.

Woody Allen, shown here with Diane Keaton, is one of those fortunate people who can write, direct, and star in his productions. Copyright 1978 by United Artists Corporation.

1977

Woody Allen
for Annie Hall

It is difficult to believe anything a comedian says about himself. It is just as difficult to believe anything another person says about a comedian. But, regardless of this, it would appear that Allen Stewart Konigsberg (AKA Woody Allen) *was* born. The great event occurred on 1 December 1935. From this point on, the facts become fuzzy, intermingling with fiction as the private Allen becomes mixed up with the public Allen. The thousands of one-lines he has thrown out about his marriages, his family, his downtrodden youth, and the indignities he has suffered have been woven into the Allen canon as gospel. It is extremely doubtful that Allen could have climbed to the top in the dog-eat-dog of show business if he is truly the shy, introverted little fellow that he tries to project.

Allen grew up in Brooklyn, did poorly in school, and decided to be a writer. He began with one-line contributions to columnists, and then went into sketch writing, becoming a staff writer at NBC when he was nineteen, working for the likes of Sid Caesar and Gary Moore. In time, a couple of enterprising agents persuaded Allen that he should be delivering his wit himself instead of putting it into the mouths of lesser men.

He caught on fast and became a top night club performer. Then, in 1964, Charles K. Feldman, an agent turned producer, caught Allen's act and decided he was just the man to rewrite a script Feldman was having trouble with. The script was *What's New, Pussycat?* Allen also had a minor role in the film.

He next took on the job of writing a soundtrack to convert a Japanese film, *What's Up, Tiger Lily?*, into an American release. This was followed by a successful Broadway play, *Don't Drink the Water*. He then was given the director's job on the film *Take the Money and Run* (1969).

Today, he is one of those fortunate movie-makers who has complete control of the films he directs and is usually the writer and star as well. After a series of profitable, but not exactly blockbusting films, he wrote (in collaboration with Marshall Brickman), directed, and starred in *Annie Hall*, the 1977 Oscar winner for best picture. It earned his costar, Diane Keaton, a best actress award, as well as bringing Allen the best director's Oscar.

In the course of rising from a standup night club comedian to a triple-threat movie maker, Allen acquired and discarded a couple of wives. Then he met Diane Keaton who appeared in the stage version of *Play It Again, Sam* with him. They moved in together for a year and then separated, although still remaining the best of friends.

Annie Hall (Hall is Keaton's real surname) is a fictionalized account of this romance between Allen and Miss Keaton. It is the story of two neurotic people. Allen described it as the story of a man of forty who reexamines his life and his relationship with a girl who has left him for a record promoter, trying to figure out what went wrong with a relationship that at first seemed just right.

Both Miss Keaton and Allen have admitted that there is a lot of truth in the film, although neither has been much help in letting us know which is true and which is make-believe.

Allen did make it plain that their separation did not come because of another man as it was portrayed in the film. They just mutually decided that it would be better for her to move to her own apartment. They continued to get together for a while after that and then gradually tapered off.

Miss Keaton said only that it just happened.

Play It Again Sam had Woody Allen as a pseudo-Humphrey Bogart in the film version of Allen's earlier play. Copyright 1972 by Paramount Pictures Corporation.

Woody Allen and Diane Keaton had partially real-life roles in *Annie Hall*, which earned Oscars for both of them. Copyright 1977 by United Artists Corporation.

As a clue to what really caused the floundering of the romance, we can look at the original title of the film. It was called *Anhedonia*. If your dictionary is sufficiently unabridged, you will find this defined as a state in which nothing gives a person pleasure. This ties in with a statement Annie Hall makes in the film. She tells the Allen character: "You're an island unto yourself, like New York City. You're incapable of enjoying life." From this we can speculate that the real Woody Allen is a loner who wants something of life, but doesn't know what it is. When he grasps something that seems to be what he wants, it turns out not to be that at all.

Allen has a great comic talent. We'll have to wait to see where it leads him.

Annie Hall (1977), a Jack Rollins-Charles H. Joffe Production for United Artists Corporation release. Directed by Woody Allen. Screenplay Woody Allen and Marshall Brickman. Principal cast members: Woody Allen, Diane Keaton, Tony Roberts, Carol Kane, Shelley Duvall.

Michael Cimino (left) with Robert De Niro and Meryl Streep during filming of *The Deer Hunter*. Copyright 1978 by Universal City Studios Incorporated.

1978

Michael Cimino for The Deer Hunter

The purpose of the Academy of Motion Picture Arts and Sciences is to encourage the art of motion pictures and to recognize those who have made material contributions to it. The charter does not call for any politics or self-serving by any individual, party or creed. The academy may and should honor films, and those who produced them, that may be highly political in themselves—provided only that the film or performances were indeed the best of the year.

But to turn the academy or its annual Oscar show into a political platform for either right, left, or middle, is to begin the destruction of the academy and its famous Oscar. This can happen, because today the academy is representative of all the industry except a few rebels like George C. Scott. To turn the awards academy into a political event will alienate all those who do not subscribe to whatever "ism" is represented. There are plenty of platforms and opportunities for political dissent without turning the Oscar show into a battleground.

Marlon Brando was an early offender. In 1974, he refused the Oscar for his performance in *The Godfather* on the inappropriate premise that Hollywood had not treated the Indians right. Such actions are attempts at censorship and should be vigorously opposed by all political persuasions. From the days of Thomas Edison, when nickelodeon operators had to black out Little Egypt's bare midriff, to today when groups are still (in Riverside, California) trying to stop the showing of *The Birth of a Nation*, the movie industry has fought censorship that threatened to strangle creativity. We don't need the movie industry's joining in on the other side.

But political discord rose again when the 1978 awards were made in April 1979. Two pictures presenting opposing views of the Vietnamese War were among the contenders. Jane Fonda and Jon Voight were in *Coming Home*, about the trials of a man who had been crippled in the war. The other nominee was *The Deer Hunter*, with Robert de Niro. Both were definitely anti-war, but politically opposite, or so their critics seemed to believe.

In the final balloting, *The Deer Hunter* got awards for best picture, director, and supporting actor, plus two technical awards. *Coming Home* brought best actress and actor award to Fonda and Voight, and also won as best original screenplay.

Jane Fonda lashed out at *The Deer Hunter*, calling it racist, although she admitted that she had not seen it. Other critics joined in, claiming the Viet Cong were represented as inhuman and the prisoner torture scenes were distortions of history. A group of demonstrators showed up outside the hall where the awards were given; fighting broke out and led to thirteen arrests.

No one denied the power of the picture or its artistry. All the furor against it was directed towards its political slant and alleged departure from factual history.

Michael Cimino, the director, appeared stunned by the demonstration. Speaking to the press after the awards, Cimino said, "*The Deer Hunter* is a movie. It is not history, and it is not a newsreel. I was not trying to recreate reality. I was trying to make a movie. My critics are entitled to their accusations just as I am entitled to say what my intentions were not. I made a very simple story about people, friendship, and courage."

He went on to say that the highly controversial scene where Viet Cong torture an American prisoner with Russian roulette was simply a dramatic device. It did not symbolize anything, he said, and then added, "It was intended to move the story along. Someone once asked John Ford why he shot Indians in his pictures. He replied that without it he wouldn't be able to set up a chase."

The story ranges from life in the steel-mill towns of Pennsylvania to the horrors of jungle warfare in Viet Nam. Robert de Niro is the deer hunter of the title. His philosophy of hunting is to kill with one bullet. Teaming with two friends from the steel mills, John Savage and Christopher Walken (who got a supporting actor award), De Niro goes off to war in a burst of patriotism.

The story is told in bursts of cinematic explosions: the opening Russian Orthodox wedding, the deer hunt with its confrontation between man and beast, the controversial torture scenes in Viet Nam, a stunning river-escape scene, and the closing scene of the survivors singing "God Bless America." Considering that, of the three, De Niro came back a changed man, Savage minus an arm and his legs, and Walken not at all, many considered this final song ironic. Cimino denied it. He claimed it was a genuine expression of faith in the country.

Regardless of the controversy, *The Deer Hunter*, cinematically, was an outstanding job. It deserved its Oscar as best picture and also its other honor, the New York Film Critics' Award.

The Deer Hunter (1978), Produced by Barry Spikings, and presented by Universal Pictures and EMI Films. Directed by Michael Cimino. Screenplay by Deric Washburn, from an original story by Cimino and Washburn, with Louis Garfinkle and Quinn K. Redeker. Photographed by Vilmos Zsigmond. Principal cast members: Robert de Niro, John Savage, Christopher Walken, John Cazale, Meryl Streep.

Benton, right, with Dustin Hoffman and Stanley Jaffe, center, plan a scene for *Kramer vs Kramer*. Copyright 1979 by Columbia Pictures Industries, Inc.

1979

Robert Benton
for Kramer vs Kramer

The 52nd Academy Award presentations, held on April 14, 1980, went very smoothly. It appeared that for the first time in several years the Oscars would be presented without someone or some group using the big show to air social complaints.

But then as the recipients gathered backstage for the post-award meeting with the press, Rona Barrett of ABC-TV tried to stir up a belated controversy. She had earlier called *Kramer vs Kramer*, the winning picture, a soap opera. Dustin Hoffman, the picture's star, needled her as he came backstage by saying, "The soap opera won!"

Barrett retorted, "Many feminists and many women who have seen the film feel that the picture is in essence a slap at them because it says that one parent has to be better than the other and that this is the father."

Meryl Streep, who received a supporting actress Oscar for the film, came to Hoffman's aid. She said that she was a feminist and did not feel that way about *Kramer vs Kramer* at all. At this point soft-spoken Robert Benton, the picture's director and script writer, interrupted to defend his work.

Kramer vs Kramer, based on the novel by Avery Corman, is about an incompatible couple, Ted (Hoffman) and Joanna (Streep) who separate as the film opens. Joanna leaves their young son with his father. Ted must now learn to be a mother as well as a father to the boy (Justin Henry). Later Joanna decides she wants custody of the boy and goes to court, providing the film with its title. The judge, as most often happens in custody cases, decides for the mother. Then in a sudden reversal of character, Joanna realizes that she is not a good mother and the interests of the boy (and herself) are best served by leaving him with his father, but with her retaining visiting rights.

It was the implication that the father would make a better mother that aroused Barrett's ire. But Benton insisted that "this is not a story of a father who becomes a mother. To attack it on those grounds is not a reasonable assumption."

Benton claimed that he wanted to show the love of a father for his son. Referring to his own 13-year-old son, Benton said, "A lot of my feelings for John are in *Kramer vs Kramer*." In fact, in his thank-you speech to the audience after receiving the award, he included "my son John" among those to whom he expressed appreciation.

Robert Benton, like so many who have won director's Oscars, did not have a theatrical family background. He was born in Waxahachie, Texas, in 1933. He showed an artistic bent and received a Bachelor of Arts degree from the University of Texas. Then at 23 he became art director for *Esquire* magazine in New York. Here he put down roots for the next seven years. While at *Esquire* he got to know David Newman, a writer-editor on the staff.

The two left *Esquire* in 1963 to write a screenplay based on the life of two Texas desperados, Clyde Barrow and Bonnie Parker, who were killed by the FBI in 1933. It took them four years to sell the script. But with Warren Beatty and Faye Dunaway in the leading roles, the film, called *Bonnie and Clyde*, was one of the hits of 1967.

Benton first broke into motion pictures as co-author of the screenplay for Arthur Penn's *Bonnie and Clyde*, with Faye Dunaway and Warren Beatty. Copyright 1967 by Warner Bros. Pictures Inc.

Jeff Bridges with John Savage and Damon Cofer prepare for a holdup in Robert Benton's *Bad Company.* Copyright 1972 by Paramount Pictures Corporation and Jaffilms, Inc.

The success of *Bonnie and Clyde* brought Benton and Newman a three-picture writing contract with Warner Brothers. This did not turn out so good for the young writers. Only *There Was a Crooked Man*, directed by Joseph Mankiewicz, got produced.

At about this point, Newman decided he wanted to direct as well as write. Benton said he was of the same opinion. The two then wrote scripts for each other. The result for Benton was *Bad Company* (1972), with Jeff Bridges and Barry Brown. The story, scripted by Newman and Benton, was about two draft dodgers from the Civil War cutting capers around Kansas in 1865.

Benton's second directorial effort was *The Late Show,* with Art Carney and Bill Macy, plus Lily Tomlin, Howard Duff and others. Robert Altman produced the film for Warners. It drew excellent critical notices, but as often happens, the notices were better than ticket sales.

So it was back to script writing for Benton. Stanley Jaffe took him on to turn Avery Corman's *Kramer vs Kramer* into a screenplay for Francois Truffaut to direct. Truffaut withdrew and Jaffe decided to give the picture to Benton. As a result of this decision, Jaffe as producer, Hoffman as star, Streep as supporting actress and Benton as screenplay/adaptor and director all trooped to the stage on Oscar night to take home five awards among them.

In winning most of the major awards, *Kramer vs Kramer* had to buck competition with *Apocalypse Now,* Francis Ford Coppola's blockbuster; *Norma Rae,* which brought Sally Field the number one actress award; the science fiction *Alien,* which was recognized only for visual effects; and *All That Jazz,* Bob Fosse's fictionalized look at himself.

As to why *Kramer vs Kramer* won over such formidable competition, it may have been because Benton made his film seem so real. And for a director with only two previous pictures to his credit, Benton's technique was superb. In one interview, Hoffman spoke of telling Benton that he was drained dry after a scene. He could give no more to this particular scene. Benton just nodded as if in agreement and ordered the cameras to roll. Hoffman said all he could do then was to give more even if he thought he could not.

Kramer vs Kramer, released by Columbia Pictures Industries, Inc. Directed by Robert Benton. Screenplay by Robert Benton, from Avery Corman's novel. Nestor Almendros director of photography. Produced by Stanley R. Jaffe. Cast included Dustin Hoffman, Meryl Streep, Justin Henry, Jane Alexander.

The Late Show, with Bill Macy and Art Carney, right, was Robert Benton's second directorial effort. Copyright 1975 by Warner Bros. Inc.

Index of Illustrations

Articles *a*, *and*, and *the* in front of titles have been omitted for clarity in indexing. Only principal actors and actresses in the scenes have been identified.